Confession & Forgiveness

Professing

FAITH

as

AMBASSADORS

of

Reconciliation

Ted Kober

CONCORDIA PUBLISHING HOUSE · SAINT LOUIS

To Sonja and David,
who have forgiven me so often

Copyright © 2002 by Peacemaker Ministries.
Published by Concordia Publishing House
3558 S. Jefferson Avenue, St. Louis, MO 63118-3968
Manufactured in the United States of America.

Library of Congress Cataloging-in-Publication Data

Kober, Ted.

  Confession and forgiveness : professing faith as ambassadors of reconciliation / Ted Kober.
      p. cm.

Includes bibliographical references.

ISBN 0-7586-0063-1

    1. Reconciliation—Religious aspects—Lutheran Church—Missouri Synod. 2. Forgiveness—Religious aspects—Lutheran Church—Missouri Synod. 3. Confession—Lutheran Church—Missouri Synod. I. Title.

    BX8074 .C6 K63   2002

    234' .5--dc21   2002015604

1 2 3 4 5 6 7 8 9 10   11 10 09 08 07 06 05 04 03 02

Contents

Introduction   7

1. Called to Be Ambassadors   13
    Set an Example
    One Man's Confession Initiates Reconciliation

2. Distinguishing Reconciliation from Conflict
Resolution   19
    Reconciliation Often Makes Conflict Resolution
    Possible
    Causes of Conflict
    Foundation of All Peacemaking Found in Jesus Christ
    Addressing Both Personal and Substantive Issues
    Theological Conflicts

3. Biblical Peacemaking   33
    What Characterizes *Christian* Reconciliation?

4. The First Distinction: The Centrality of Christ   38
    Losing Sight of Christ
    Balancing Law and Gospel

5. The Second Distinction: The Responsibility
of the Church   46
    The Church's Role in My Lawsuit
    Whose Job Is It?

6. The Third Distinction: The Necessity of Biblical
Counseling   56
    The World View Versus the Biblical View
    The Significance of the Biblical View of Self-Worth
    and Identity
    Self-Assurance Leads to Self-Deception

7. The Fourth Distinction: The Comprehensiveness of God's Word 63

From the Playground to the Courtroom
For All Cultures and Times

8. Confess Your Sins to Profess Your Faith 69

Confession of Sin Proclaims Christ
Self-Righteous Defenses Deny Christ

9. Remaining Approachable 77

Unapproachable Leaders
Approachable Leaders
Do Others Perceive You as Approachable?
Known by Their Approachability
A New Creation in Christ

10. Examination of Sin 94

Is Examination of My Sin Really Necessary?
Healthy Methods for Examination
Dangers of Examination
Examination Is Not the End

11. Words That Lead to Salvation and Life 118

Words of Confession
Words of Forgiveness
When Should I Forgive?

12. Professing Faith in Private Confession and Forgiveness 138

Mutual Confession and Forgiveness
Private Confession to a Fellow Believer
Individual Confession and Absolution from Your Pastor
Family Confession and Absolution
Requirements for Hearers of Confession

13. Professing Faith in Public Confession and
   Forgiveness   159

   Corporate Confession and Forgiveness
   Individual Public Confession and Forgiveness
   When Individual Public Confession Is Appropriate
   What about Consequences?

14. Reconciliation: Not Just an Event   170

Appendix A: The Peacemaker's Pledge   173

Appendix B: Questions for Examination   175

Appendix C: Words of Absolution from Scripture   181

Appendix D: Holy Absolution (With Your Pastor)   183

Appendix E: A Wedding Prayer of Confession and
Forgiveness   185

Appendix F: Family Confession and Forgiveness   186

Bibliography   189

Other Resources   191

Introduction

Pastor Schmitt led his church in a way that surprised everyone in the room. Our peacemaking team had just completed delivering our final oral report to the leadership of this conflicted church, and we invited anyone to respond to the presentation. We were uncertain how people might react, including the pastor.

Pastor Schmitt rose first to speak. Trembling, he slowly unfolded a piece of yellow legal paper he had pulled out of his pocket. He introduced his statement by acknowledging that he was personally responsible for contributing to many of the conflicts in their church. He read his prepared admission, clearly confessing his sins without excuse.

The room fell silent as Pastor Schmitt identified specific examples of his public sins. He admitted his own denial of his contributions to many of the disputes. He described running away from dealing with others by keeping an extremely busy work schedule. He confessed his defensive attitude toward people who brought complaints, and he acknowledged that he specifically made confronting him difficult and uncomfortable. Pastor Schmitt avoided using words such as *but* or *maybe*, which can be used to excuse one's actions instead of confessing them. He promised to amend his sinful life, asking one of his most ardent opponents to help hold him accountable to his good intentions. He expressed his desire to personally be reconciled to those who were angry with him. Finally, he asked for forgiveness from his lay leaders and fellow church workers.

His fellow leaders sat stunned. When he finished reading, he started to return to his chair. I gently stopped him, indicating that we were not yet done. I invited the rest of the group to respond to their pastor's confession with the Good News of the Gospel, using the familiar words of the Declaration of Grace from their Sunday morning worship service (*Lutheran Worship*, p. 159). Normally, these words of absolution—as indicated in the liturgy—are pronounced by a "called and ordained servant of the Word.") Tears filled Pastor Schmitt's eyes as he heard members of his flock proclaim God's forgiveness for him.

I then invited individual responses to Pastor Schmitt. One by one, key leaders spoke personal forgiveness to their pastor. Then Bob, one of the pastor's most outspoken critics, began to speak. Bob personally expressed his forgiveness and then began to stumble over words of his own confession for mistreating Pastor. But Pastor Schmitt did not wait for Bob to struggle over his words. This pastor reached out to his former enemy, motioning for him to stand, and they hugged each other with tears, sharing words of personal forgiveness.

Pastor Schmitt's unusual act of leadership prompted several others to publicly acknowledge their sins against one another. After each confession, the assembly responded with absolution, and individuals also publicly pronounced personal forgiveness. Following these public confessions, we provided these Christian brothers and sisters the opportunity to privately seek out those in the room with whom they had unresolved issues. Many reconciled their relationships with mutual confession and forgiveness. All over the church one could hear crying and laughing among people who months before had stopped talking to one another.

Confession and forgiveness among God's people were never intended to be reserved for an isolated reconciliation event for those engulfed in intense conflict. For the Christian, confession and forgiveness are a way of life, something we do in our normal, everyday lives. Children of God who regularly confess sins and forgive others demonstrate strong faith in Christ and model Christian leadership for the church. Such leaders are ambassadors of reconciliation.

In this book I desire to help equip you in your vocation as an ambassador of reconciliation. God uses various people to lead others—pastors, teachers, elders, church officers, parents—and many others who may not be "officially appointed" but serve as examples for others. I could have written about the entire spectrum of reconciliation and conflict resolution, but I chose to focus on the key elements of confession and forgiveness. Although we acknowledge that this subject is rather basic to our faith, for most of us confession and forgiveness are rarely easy or routinely practiced in life's daily struggles. Nonetheless, when applied consistently in the life of a Christian leader, this one fundamental of the sanctified life makes a profound difference in influencing believers and nonbelievers.

I approach this from the perspective of our charge to be ambassadors of reconciliation. We will review the primary cause of conflict and its relationship to the ministry of reconciliation. We'll explore what makes biblical peacemaking distinctly Christian and unique from all other conflict resolution models. Our study will reinforce the relationship between confessing our sins and professing our faith and the necessity for daily contrition. Included will be reflection on our witness to believers and unbelievers as we respond to conflict, especially noting the influence that leaders have in modeling confession or self-righteous attitudes. A related topic will deal with the approachability of church leaders.

Our human nature frequently doubts the power of God's work in the challenges of everyday living, and we sometimes are unable to comprehend the many ways in which the Gospel can be applied in our personal lives. Thus, I illustrate many of the concepts drawn from Scripture with examples of actual events ranging from biblical times to contemporary settings. True-life stories can inspire us and help us appreciate what God does for us and intends for us to do. I have changed names and other details to protect confidences, so please do not assume you know the people or particulars of a specific case. (When I make presentations, occasionally someone suggests that they knew the original parties from my illustrations, but it turns out otherwise. Because we all suffer from the same human nature, true-life situations repeat themselves in various places with different people.) The accounts of my interactions with my family and pastors are true, and I appreciate my family and pastors for allowing me to share these private experiences with you.

In the appendix I have provided some resources to help you apply the ideas presented. I also encourage you to check out the references and other resources for more information.

I pray that this book will be a blessing to you, your family, and the people God brings around you as you live out your vocation as Christ's ambassador.

"Let the words of my mouth and the meditation of my heart be acceptable in your sight, O LORD, my rock and my redeemer" (Psalm 19:14 ESV).

1

Called to Be Ambassadors

Every Christian is called by God to serve as an ambassador of reconciliation. Sinners who begin to grasp the seriousness of their plight treasure the Good News that God reconciled us to Himself while we were yet sinners (Romans 5:8). Who is better qualified to tell others about this great find than those who need it most? So, God chose us, forgiven sinners, to serve as His representatives in delivering this lifesaving message. St. Paul wrote to the Christians in Corinth:

> So from now on we regard no one from a worldly point of view. Though we once regarded Christ in this way, we do so no longer. Therefore, if anyone is in Christ, he is a new creation; the old has gone, the new has come! All this is from God, who reconciled us to Himself through Christ and gave us the ministry of reconciliation: that God was reconciling the world to Himself in Christ, not counting men's sins against them. And He has committed to us the message of reconciliation. We are therefore Christ's ambassadors, as though God were making His appeal through us. We implore you on Christ's behalf: Be reconciled to God. God made Him who had no sin to be sin for us, so that

> in Him we might become the righteousness of
> God. (2 Corinthians 5:16–21)

Notice that the message of reconciliation is salutary not only for unbelievers but also for believers. Yes, God's people need to be continually forgiven, strengthened, and encouraged by hearing that eternally sweet news that we are His chosen ones, brought near to Him through the blood of His own Son. It is this Gospel message that moves us to respond to God's love in kind. As St. Paul proclaims in verses 14–15, our Savior's love is our motivation:

> For Christ's love compels us, because we are con-
> vinced that one died for all, and therefore all died.
> And He died for all, that those who live should no
> longer live for themselves but for Him who died
> for them and was raised again. (2 Corinthians
> 5:14–15)

Leaders in Christ's church enjoy the privilege and bear a responsibility to equip other saints as ambassadors of reconciliation. They disciple God's children through preaching and teaching, by mediating disputes among believers and encouraging them to be reconciled to one another, and by managing the congregation's organizational affairs in a way that is consistent with God's ministry of reconciliation. But perhaps the most important way that leaders disciple ambassadors is by example.

Set an Example

St. Paul urged the young church leader Timothy:

"Don't let anyone look down on you because you are young, but set an example for the believers in speech, in life, in love, in faith and in purity" (1 Timothy 4:12).

As a father and husband, I continue to be amazed how my son and wife are much more likely to imitate my actual behavior (good, bad, and indifferent) over time than all the pompous speeches and corrections that I can deliver with my tongue. People learn in many ways, but our example is our most effective sermon.

Since this book is designed to help prepare you as a Christian leader, my focus is to encourage you to be a "Timothy." Set an example that the believers in your church and family can follow. Be an ambassador of the message of reconciliation.

I fully expect that you will fail in your attempts to be a good model, just as I do. Why? You and I fail because we are not only saints, we are also sinners. No matter how much we want to please and honor our Lord by keeping His commands, we miss the mark every day. But because of God's great grace and mercy, we are forgiven every day, and we can give tremendous witness to our faith by trusting in that forgiveness and confessing our sins. Actually, it is from our reactions to our own failures that other sinners learn most.

Thus, this book features stories about leaders who faltered. Many of them came back to the foot of the cross to find personal comfort and strength and were compelled by Christ's love to be an example to others. Confession and forgiveness brought healing to them in the conflicts of their everyday lives. In our weakness Christ's power and love shine brightest (see 2 Corinthians 11:29–30; 12:9). Some of them, however, struggled to put their faith in action.

Think of some of the great heroes of the Bible—people such as Moses, King David, Jonah, Jesus' disciples, the persecutor Saul who later became known as Paul. Are they heroes because of their own self-acclaimed righteousness and their perfect obedience? Or do we admire them because in their failings they gave witness to their faith, turning back to God and seeking His forgiveness? Moses, whom God chose for a special purpose, granting him extraordinary faith and authority, frequently whined to God about his calling, sometimes in anger. Moreover, he blatantly disobeyed God when he struck the rock at Meribah Kadesh instead of speaking to it for water (Numbers 20:1–13). King David, beloved of God, was anointed as king over Israel. Yet he committed adultery with Bathsheba and then arranged for the death of her husband, Uriah, in an attempt to cover up her pregnancy (2 Samuel 11). God called His prophet Jonah to preach repentance to the Ninevites, but Jonah ran away because he feared the Ninevites might repent and receive God's mercy (Jonah 1). Jesus' disciples repeatedly argued among themselves as to who was the greatest, even while they were with Him (Mark 9:33–34; 10:35–45). They even vied for top honors at the Last Supper (Luke 22:24)! When Jesus was arrested at Gethsemane, His "faithful" disciples fled, and even Peter, the "rock," adamantly denied knowing Jesus (Mark 14:50, 66–72). Saul zealously pursued the persecution of Christians to eradicate this growing movement (Acts 9:1–2).

Should we honor these sinful failures as sainted

leaders of God's people? What makes their example so important not only to the people of their day but also to us? When in their weak moments they floundered, these leaders trusted God. Through repentance and confession, they clung to their Redeemer and found the joy of salvation in the forgiveness of sins.

Such biblical heroes serve us as ambassadors of reconciliation. They trusted God and His promises and received forgiveness. They proclaimed this Good News to others, and their professions of faith continue to inspire us today.

One Man's Confession Initiates Reconciliation

I provided consultation for a conflicted congregation that was controlled by a few strong leaders. Kevin chaired the board of trustees for 20 years, and he exercised substantial influence throughout the church. Arising from disagreements over the elders' dismissal of the pastor, he initiated a petition drive to fire the entire board of elders. In his zeal for what he believed was a righteous cause, Kevin widely distributed some seething letters. He accused all the elders, called them some filthy names, and made strong declarations about their wicked motives. He neglected to speak directly with those he opposed, and some of his assumptions and "facts" were grossly erroneous. In his anger, Kevin sinned.

After some counseling, prayer, and study in God's Word, Kevin recognized his sin. Even though he still disagreed with the final outcome and the manner in which the pastor was removed, he acknowledged that others' actions did not justify his own sin. Kevin prepared a written confession that he personally read to the elders, asking for their forgiveness. Shocked, the elders hesitated, unsure how to respond. Finally, one of them expressed personal forgiveness, and the others followed. With the elder board's approval, Kevin distributed a summary of his confession and the elders' response of forgiveness to the original recipients of his letters.

Kevin's example stirred the elders to meet privately and prepare their own confession, which they read to the congregation in the Sunday service. An amazing demonstration of the reconciliation occurred when the elders nominated Kevin to join their board. An entire congregation experienced healing from reconciliation, sparked by one man's confession of sin, the offering of forgiveness from his enemies, and the elders' response of public confession.

Kevin and the elders are first of all recipients of God's reconciliation. Their personal confession of sin and granting of forgiveness made them ambassadors of reconciliation. Their dynamic example left a lasting impression on the other members of that congregation, many of whom grew in faith to be reconciled with former opponents.

2

Distinguishing Reconciliation from Conflict Resolution

What is the difference between "reconciliation" and "conflict resolution"?

Divorce resolves conflict, but it fails to bring reconciliation. A judge issues his decision on a lawsuit and resolves the conflict, but the parties remain unreconciled. A man quits his job because he cannot handle the constant bickering with co-workers. His resignation brings resolution for himself, but he forfeits reconciliation with former friends. A congregational president and his wife transfer their memberships to a neighboring church to remove themselves from the fray. Both congregation and couple believe that this resolves the problem, but reconciliation never takes place.

Sin separates us from God. "But your iniquities have separated you from your God; your sins have hidden His face from you, so that He will not hear" (Isaiah 59:2). By nature we are enemies of God. This conflict is resolved when justice is delivered. The sentence? Eternal separation from God in hell.

From God, do you want *conflict resolution* or *reconciliation?* Can you have *both?*

May we eternally praise our heavenly Father, who chose reconciliation to resolve our conflict! Our sin broke our relationship with God. But while we were still His enemies, He reconciled us to Himself through Christ. Justice was satisfied with Jesus' painful death on the cross. His resurrection assures us that He defeated sin, death, and the devil, and those who believe in God's promise of forgiveness will live eternally in heaven because we have been reconciled to God.

Our broken relationship to God was perfectly healed in Jesus, through whom we have forgiveness. We receive this forgiveness when we repent and believe this Good News. Reconciliation with one another comes also through confession and forgiveness.

Conflict resolution is important. We ought to strive to reach mutually satisfying solutions to our disagreements. Sometimes working to resolve conflict can help parties also reach reconciliation. In other situations, the best solution attainable might be conflict resolution without reconciliation.

But absence of reconciliation leaves broken relationships. Reconciliation is essential in our relationship to God and in our relationships to other people. The lack of restored relationships can lead to eternal consequences.

Reconciliation Often Makes Conflict Resolution Possible

Mark, a Christian vendor, brought charges against an international ministry for refusing to pay a significant part of his fee. Susan, the ministry's chief financial officer, claimed that she had paid all appropriate amounts, according to their attorney's interpretation of the contract. The two parties were more than $60,000 apart. They requested a Christian arbitrator from Peacemaker Ministries to judge the matter, in accord with Scripture, rather than go to court in a lawsuit. Each claimed that there were no personal issues to reconcile. From both of their perspectives, they simply disagreed over the interpretation of the contract and requested help for resolving this one issue.

Peacemaker Ministries encouraged the two sides to first attempt resolution through mediation so that the opportunity for reconciliation could be realized. With arbitration, they were advised, reconciliation was much less likely.

In mediation an impartial mediator facilitates negotiation of material issues and encourages reconciliation of personal issues through mutual confession and forgiveness. The parties retain all rights to settle their own disputes and reach agreement. As the two sides present their stories, the mediator helps them to identify both material and personal issues. The Christian mediator reminds them of Christ's love and forgiveness of their sins, and he admonishes them to respond to God's love in their actions toward one another to move toward reconciliation.

In arbitration the parties give up their right to make their own decisions, and they empower the arbitrator to act as a judge who hears the two sides' stories and issues a binding decision. In such settings the parties are much less likely to admit personal fault or forgive their opponent because they attempt to convince the arbitrator of the rightness of their positions. In addition, an arbitrator cannot decide issues of the heart. For example, he cannot issue a decision to force a party to confess sin, forgive sin, or show love. He can only judge on substantive issues.

Mark and the international ministry, represented by Susan, reluctantly agreed to try mediation, provided that the mediator could be later appointed as their arbitrator and issue a decision for them if they were unable to reach voluntary settlement. I was appointed as their mediator/arbitrator.

The mediation took nearly 12 hours. We spent the first 10 hours addressing the personal issues that they claimed didn't exist. Once Mark and Susan reconciled their personal issues through mutual confession and forgiveness, they were able to quickly reach agreement on the $60,000 difference in 90 minutes. After they forgave one another, their restored trust and respect for one another made negotiation on the material issues much easier. Arbitration became unnecessary. Reconciliation made conflict resolution possible.

While these two parties were satisfied with the settlement, Mark and Susan rejoiced over the restoration of their personal relationship. As they celebrated reconciliation and others in their respective organizations learned about it, they served as Christ's ambassadors, giving glory to God for the ministry of reconciliation found in Jesus Christ and the forgiveness of sin.

Causes of Conflict

Ken Sande, in "The Peacemaker Seminar," defines conflict as "a difference in opinion or purpose that frustrates someone's goals or desires." These differences can range from minor disagreements such as what television program will be watched to more major disputes that result in divorce, termination of employment, or lawsuits.

What causes conflict? Many factors contribute to conflict. Misunderstandings produce confusion that leads to disagreements. Differences in values, goals, priorities, and missions clash, often resulting in disputes. Competition over limited resources creates strife.

Nevertheless, the primary cause of conflict is identified for us in Scripture as sinful desires that lead to sinful words and actions. St. James states very plainly:

> What causes fights and quarrels among you? Don't they come from your desires that battle within you? You want something but don't get it. You kill and covet, but you cannot have what you want. You quarrel and fight. You do not have, because you do not ask God. When you ask, you do not receive, because you ask with wrong motives, that you may spend what you get on your pleasures. (James 4:1–3)

Sin is the major cause of conflict in our life. Even when sin is not the initial cause, it does not take long before two sinners in disagreement respond to one another in sinful ways. Our basic desires to control others, our underlying nature to serve ourselves first, and our driving force to be gods of our own destinies bring us in conflict with God and with others.

In the story above about Mark and Susan, both people claimed that their dispute was simply a misunderstanding of their oral and written agreements. Neither party admitted that personal relationship issues were involved. However, as I mentioned above, we spent the bulk of the mediation dealing with those personal sin issues that they said didn't exist. What were those issues? Put yourself in their positions for a moment, and imagine what happened.

When the dispute first arose, it could be correctly defined as a misunderstanding in contract interpretation. But as the conflict escalated and emotions increased, sinful desires led them to sinful words and actions. Mark became defensive and persistent in contacting Susan. Susan quickly tired of what she perceived as petty complaints, and she instructed her assistant to take messages whenever he called. Mark became angry and began to berate Susan's assistant with accusations against Susan. When the assistant became frustrated at being caught in the middle, Susan directed that Mark's calls be transferred to other department heads. Then, in a management meeting, Susan broadly announced her judgment of Mark's behavior as unchristian. Mark became aware of his being shoved around and of Susan's warnings to her co-workers, and Mark responded by telling other clients about the ungodly behavior exhibited by top officials of this well-known ministry.

Did you follow the progression? The misunderstanding led these two people to respond to their disagreement in sinful ways: denial, avoidance, and attacking by speaking to others about each other rather than to each other honestly and directly. In their zeal to serve their own interests, they sought to bring hurt to the other person.

But when they were given the opportunity to express their personal hurts, Mark and Susan began to understand how they had sinned against God and against one another. Their "hidden" anger against one another actually prevented them from resolving their dispute because they had no relationship left in which they could trust one another in negotiation. Reconciliation of the sin issues rebuilt a trust that allowed them to resolve their financial disagreement.

Foundation of All Peacemaking Found in Jesus Christ

If we deny the sin issues of a conflict, we are likely to circumvent reconciliation through confession and forgiveness because we focus on simply solving the material problem. We choose to ignore the sin factor because that would mean we admit that we are sinners. We once again fail. Our human frailty is exposed before God and others.

Fortunately for us, God did not choose to deny the sin issues of our conflicts. Our most serious conflict is with God. Sinful human beings are by nature God's enemies. But in St. Paul's Letter to the Romans, we read, "Therefore, since we have been justified through faith, we have peace with God through our Lord Jesus Christ.

. . . God demonstrates His own love for us in this: While we were yet sinners, Christ died for us" (Romans 5:1–8).

All true peacemaking is based on the foundation of what God has done for us in Christ Jesus. Because we have been reconciled to God, we have been given a gift to share with others: forgiveness.

God holds an active interest in all our conflicts. He was so interested in our conflicts and the sins that cause them that He sent His only begotten Son to take the punishment of our sins. Through our reconciliation with God, we have been given the privilege to be proclaimers of that same reconciliation to those with whom we are in conflict. We celebrate that Good News when we speak forgiveness to one another and when we confess our sins to one another.

Addressing Both Personal and Substantive Issues

Although reconciliation of our personal issues is achieved through confession and forgiveness, substantive (or material) issues are resolved through other means, including extensive conversation, negotiation, mediation, or arbitration. Personal issues involve the sinful thoughts, words, and actions of disputing parties. As mentioned above, most of our conflicts are either initiated by sin or aggravated by sin, and thus personal issues must be addressed when working with most conflicts.

However, reconciling personal issues does not automatically resolve the substantive issues. Substantive issues may include systems issues, competition over limited resources, differing values and beliefs, and other material issues.

Systems issues may include disputes over prescribed policies, bylaws, rules, or clear definitions of authority. For example, a systems issue arises when two managers who share overlapping responsibilities for one employee disagree on whether or not to terminate him. Even though the two managers may reconcile through confession and forgiveness, they still need to decide whether or not to retain or release the employee, or exercise some other option.

Competition over limited resources may involve finances, human resources, and even physical spaces. For example, the pastor may schedule a wedding on the same day that the trustees arrange for a painter to stain the ceiling of the church. The pastor and trustees may discover that they did not communicate well, and they may reconcile their personal oversights. Nevertheless, the problem of having a wedding on the same day the contractor is staining must be dealt with.

When parties disagree on whether it is appropriate for a Christian woman to have an abortion, they have a value-and-belief issue. When a Christian school teacher is terminated, a material issue may include whether or not a severance package should be offered and what it should include. These differences do not disappear when the parties achieve personal reconciliation. They must be addressed.

Such substantive issues cannot be simply ignored or assumed instantly resolved just because reconciliation occurs through confession and forgiveness. While people most often fail to recognize and reconcile the personal issues in a conflict, sometimes others focus solely on the personal issues and deny that substantive issues exist or need to be resolved.

When people simply suggest that a conflict is only about substantive issues, as in the story about Mark and Susan, they miss the opportunity for reconciliation. But if they focus only on the personal issues and deny the substantive matters, they will still fail to bring closure to the dispute. Denial is a sinful response to conflict, because it prevents us from seeking to serve one another's interests and God's interests. If one party claims the problem is over personal issues and the opposing party believes that the major concern is primarily material, the truth is that the dispute really involves both personal and substantive issues. Both must be addressed for complete reconciliation and resolution.

To illustrate, consider a husband and wife who believe their conflict involves different types of issues. The wife says that there are only relational (or personal) issues to resolve. She perceives that there are no substantive issues in their marriage, but has concluded that if they only treated one another better, everything would be fine. The husband insists that their marriage difficulty has nothing to do with relationship but has everything to do with material issues. He explains that his wife overspends their budget by charging items on the credit card when they have no funds to pay for anything, and he claims that she spoils the children when they require more discipline. Both are correct in identifying part of the issues, but both err because they deny that the conflict includes both personal and substantive issues.

Personal and substantive issues arise in the church, too, especially in the area of theological conflict.

Theological Conflicts

In the church there will be times when disagreements and conflict arise over what God's Word teaches. These theological conflicts are, according to Scripture, something that is a part of church life. St. Paul teaches, "For there must be factions among you in order that those who are genuine among you may be recognized" (1 Corinthians 11:19 RSV). And again, "I urge you, brothers, to watch out for those who cause divisions and put obstacles in your way that are contrary to the teaching you have learned. Keep away from them" (Romans 16:17). In the same vein, Walther says:

> The most difficult and arduous [task] of all, beyond question, is the task of proclaiming the pure doctrine of the Gospel of Christ and at the same time exposing, refuting, and rejecting teachings that are contrary to the Gospel. The minister who does this will discover by practical experience the truth of the old saying: *Veritas odium parit* (telling the truth makes enemies). (P. 265)

Although in the church we always desire to be at peace with one another, we find that the simple task of pursuing the truth of God's Word can create conflict. As Jesus Himself says, "I did not come to bring peace, but a sword" (Matthew 10:34). In such cases, it is important for believers to recognize that theological conflicts most often include both personal and substantive issues. One harmful way people deal with theological conflict in the church is to ignore the substantive issues of theological disagreements by assuming that theological conflict is really only personal conflict. On the other hand, others may create additional controversy by pretending that only doctrinal issues and no personal issues are involved in theological conflict.

In the midst of debating and working through a disagreement over what God's Word teaches, all parties involved will be tempted to speak about one another inappropriately and to engage in behaviors and conducts that are sinful. This aspect of theological conflict can often be confused with the substantive theological issue itself. It is necessary to deal with the personal conflict in the midst of theological conflict so that the important substantive issue—the disagreements over doctrine—can be dealt with in a God-pleasing manner.

With theological conflict and disagreement, there are two extremes to avoid. First, we must avoid giving the impression that theological disagreements can or should be solved simply by dealing with the personal conflict that will inevitably accompany theological disagreements. Pure doctrine—and care for that doctrine—is an essential part of remaining faithful to our Lord. Second, we must avoid the temptation to ignore the personal aspects of theological conflict. It is too easy for human beings to wrap themselves up in the theological conflict and use it to excuse sinful behaviors and manners of dealing with one another.

Because parties in theological conflict take their faith seriously, they often become emotionally charged in defending their positions. Each man convinces himself that he is defending God's truth, and thus is tempted to arrogantly assume that he is an infallible interpreter of God's Word. This leads people to justify any means necessary, even sinful words and actions, to defend their position. However, using sinful means to protect doctrinal purity violates the very doctrine that pious people intend to defend.

For the sake of Christ's church and for the witness to unbelievers, theological disagreement must be addressed in a biblically faithful manner. The truth of God's Word is at stake in theological conflict, and this ought never be minimized or otherwise ignored. Nevertheless, all parties involved in a theological disagreement must also avoid ignoring the personal conflict that arises in the midst of theological conflict.

As parties attempt to identify the substantive issues, however, they must also strive to identify real differences. As is true in all conflicts, misunderstandings sometimes separate parties. When they finally come together and reconcile personal differences and begin to rebuild trust, they may discover that some of the differences were not as significant as they originally surmised. They may also come to realize that more serious differences exist in areas they had not previously acknowledged. Thus, an important step in resolving any type of substantive issue involves clearly identifying actual differences as well as agreements.

It is not the purpose of this book to describe the various methods for dealing with material theological conflicts or other substantive issues in a conflict (see "Other Resources" at the end of this book for more information on this subject). It is the intention of this book to help Christians be ambassadors of Christ's reconciling forgiveness in disputes. They will do this in any situation in which there is disagreement and conflict between Christians. Working to reconcile personal differences helps facilitate the hard work of resolving the substantive issues. As personal relationships are built and trust begins to grow, honest discussions can help draw out the actual material differences. Misunderstandings can be overcome, and underlying issues can be revealed. Likewise, sometimes working through some of the substantive issues may help lead people to personal reconciliation. As parties work together and see how some agreements can be reached, they sometimes soften their hearts toward one another and reach out in acts of confession and forgiveness. How Christians resolve their conflicts, theological and otherwise, speaks loudly of the faith they profess to believers and unbelievers.

3

Biblical Peacemaking

Throughout God's Word, He instructs us on living in peace with God and with others. Therefore, we turn to Scripture for hope in Jesus Christ and for living the sanctified life.

Well-meaning Christians sometimes point to Matthew 18:15–18 as God's final word on peacemaking. Jesus Himself gave us these instructions:

> If your brother sins against you, go and show him his fault, just between the two of you. If he listens to you, you have won your brother over. But if he will not listen, take one or two others along, so that "every matter may be established by the testimony of two or three witnesses." If he refuses to listen to them, tell it to the church; and if he refuses to listen even to the church, treat him as you would a pagan or tax collector. I tell you the truth, whatever you bind on earth will be bound in heaven, and whatever you loose on earth will be loosed in heaven.

Certainly this teaching from Jesus gives us specific instruction on how to deal with those who sin against us. But living in peace with others involves more than going to those who sin against us. Most often, there is sin on both sides of the dispute, and Scripture provides direction for dealing with both sides, whether or not one believes that he is guilty of sin.

In his book *The Peacemaker: A Biblical Guide to Resolving Personal Conflict* Ken Sande summarizes all that Scripture teaches about personal peacemaking in four principles, which he calls the "Four G's" (pp. 10–11):

- Glorify God.

- Get the log out of your eye.

- Go and show your brother his fault.

- Go and be reconciled.

These four principles contain the direction given us in Matthew 18, but they also take into account the many other references where God teaches personal peacemaking. In "Glorify God," we remember what role God plays in our dispute. The Christian considers the conflict as an opportunity to bring God glory and to give witness to what God has done for us through Christ. In "Get the log out of your eye," we examine our hearts to identify our individual contributions to the conflict so that we may then respond to the conflict through repentance and confession. "Go and show your brother his fault" reminds us to go directly to someone who has sinned to confront him in love rather than judge him and talk about him behind his back. We are reminded in "Go and be reconciled" that peacemaking is not passive but requires action. Jesus directs us to initiate reconciliation, forgiving others as God through Christ forgives us. An expanded description of the "Four G's" is contained in "The Peacemaker's Pledge," which can be found in Appendix A of this book.

The benefit of the "Four G's" is that they quickly

remind us of God's directions for making peace. In my life the "Four G's" have become a symbol to remember the commands of my God in loving others (Deuteronomy 6:6–9) and to recall them when I find myself in conflict.

Especially useful for me is the second G, "Get the log out of your eye," taken from Jesus' words in Matthew 7:3–5. It is so easy for me to see someone else's faults, but I am often totally blind to my own. Just recently I became angry with my son David for something he had done, and I immediately called him on the phone to ream him out and demand that he return home. In my anger I said sinful words. As I hung up the phone, I justified my sinful words to my wife because I was so unhappy with my son's error. After all, I am his father, responsible for correcting him and making him understand how he should act! The reality is that David's sin did not justify my sin, no matter what the offense. Taking Jesus' words to heart, when David arrived home, I first confessed my sin to him, asking for his forgiveness, explaining that his offense did not justify my sinful words. My son was already convicted of his sin. Reconciliation came quickly, and the rest of our discussion worked out a reasonable solution without any more shouting. It sounds simple, but it sure wasn't easy for a proud father to confess his sin to his guilty son! Remembering the second G helped me to "get the log out of my own eye."

What Characterizes *Christian* Reconciliation?

In peacemaking, even non-Christians can follow the fundamental principles described by the "Four G's." Although corrupted by sin, the human conscience bears the footprints of God's commandments. In spite of post-modernists' claims, most people believe that there is some absolute truth on which morality is based. Everyone can benefit from going directly to a person with whom one is in conflict, admitting faults and forgiving others.

Can non-Christians really adopt *biblical* peacemaking? While atheists may not be focused on glorifying God in conflict, they certainly want to be viewed by others as being reasonable people. On the other hand, many religious people, such as Muslims, Jews, or Hindus, may indeed want to glorify their gods in the way they handle their disputes. Most religions promote obedience to a god or many gods and encourage loving acts toward other people. So, if most people can accept basic biblical principles as helpful, what makes the ministry of reconciliation distinctly Christian?

St. Peter wrote, "Live such good lives among the pagans that, though they accuse you of doing wrong, they may see your good deeds and glorify God on the day He visits us" (1 Peter 2:12). Can the way we respond to our daily conflicts serve as opportunities to "live such good lives among the pagans"? Are there ways to handle conflict that reveal some significant differences between Christians and nonbelievers?

As beneficiaries of the ministry of reconciliation, we approach conflict with a spirit that is unique from the world's view of conflict. Ambassadors of this good news have become new creatures. Adopted and forgiven by God in the waters of Baptism, our Old Adam is drowned, and we have put on the new man in Christ. Building on the foundation that all peacemaking is found in Jesus Christ, Christian reconciliation features aspects not found in other methodologies for making peace.

In *Guiding People Through Conflict,* Ken Sande and I identify four characteristics that distinguish Christian peacemaking from other conflict resolution systems available in the world today: the centrality of Christ, the responsibility of the church, the necessity of biblical counseling, and the comprehensiveness of God's Word (pp. 19–21). Ambassadors of reconciliation glorify God and profess a living witness to Christ when they apply these distinctions in their lives.

4

The First Distinction: The Centrality of Christ

The first characteristic that distinguishes the ministry of reconciliation from other dispute resolution systems is the centrality of Christ. For Christian leaders, Christ *is* at the center of all our work together, or it *is not* Christian. While we might easily nod in agreement at that statement, living out this truth is far more difficult. Let me give you an example where I judged someone else on this point, while at the time I was guilty of the same thing.

Losing Sight of Christ

It happened when I attended Jack's memorial service. Jack died after a year-long battle with cancer. Since he didn't attend church, Jack's family asked the hospital chaplain to conduct the service. The chaplain explained that he ministered to Jack in the hospital, and I hoped that Jack came to know Jesus through the chaplain's hospital visits.

However, the chaplain's words lacked true comfort. His message focused on Jack and his good deeds. Observing noble traits from Proverbs, he documented Jack's achievements: a faithful husband, a dedicated father, a productive worker, and a decent golfer. Now in heaven, the chaplain declared, Jack awaited friends and family. He recited Psalm 23, prayed for Jack's soul, and led the assembly in the Lord's Prayer. From an unbeliever's viewpoint, it appeared to be a Christian funeral for a good man.

One phrase mentioned Jesus: "In Jesus' name we pray. Amen." We did not hear the reality that all men have sinned and deserve eternal death. Not once did the chaplain comfort the listeners with the Good News of the Gospel. No assurance conveyed the hope of eternal life because of Jesus' death and resurrection. And yet, he attempted to comfort the mourners with biblical texts.

We can identify "biblical truths" but fail to speak truthfully when we leave out Christ. We can even quote Scripture, as the chaplain did, but still miss the Good News about Jesus. It was easy for me to be critical of the hospital chaplain who should have known better, but I soon remembered that I had also missed an opportunity to share God's whole truth with Jack and his friends.

A few years earlier Jack had invited me to speak at a business luncheon about resolving conflicts without litigation. I accepted his invitation and presented biblical peacemaking basics including *get the log out of your own eye*, *go and show your brother his fault*, and *go and be reconciled*. I affirmed the values of confession and forgiveness. Nevertheless, I was careful not to offend anyone in this secular setting, especially Jack, by clearly and specifically talking about Jesus. Instead, I presented biblical principles for resolving conflict, telling the story of how another businessman and I settled a nasty lawsuit through mediation. Everything I said was *true*—except that I neglected to point to Christ as the foundation for all true peacemaking. I minimized how Christ's forgiveness moved me to confess my own sin to my brother and forgive him as God forgave me. Just like the apostle Peter, I hid my relationship to Jesus because of my fear of man. "Fear of man will prove to be a snare, but whoever trusts in the Lord is kept safe" (Proverbs 29:25). In my desire to receive the approval of people, I ignored the source of my strength, and I glorified my own actions of following the Bible's moral platitudes.

What a hypocrite I had been! I publicly presented peacemaking based on biblical principles but omitted the Prince of Peace. I ignored my Savior, who suffered and died for my sins, so that I could win approval of people I hardly knew.

In many ways, my message was no different than the hospital chaplain's. We both referenced Scripture as a guide for good living. We quoted God's Word and convinced ourselves that we proclaimed a Christian message. In reality we mishandled God's Word by disregarding the sacrificial death of Jesus Christ as the one and only Savior of the world, our only hope. Instead of highlighting *The Truth,* we overlooked Him. Jesus declares, "I am the way and the truth and the life. No one comes to the Father except through Me" (John 14:6). To speak biblically is to reveal—not conceal—Jesus as *The Truth.*

Satan originated half-truths. He cited the Scriptures, taking certain texts out of context, to tempt Jesus in the desert, but Jesus correctly used the Word to defeat the deceiver. Censoring the Gospel, intended or not, represses the truth.

Balancing Law and Gospel

As I work with conflicted parties today, I intentionally point to Christ as the source of true peacemaking. Sometimes Christians mentally roll their eyes as I begin to recite familiar passages of God's work of reconciliation. Many parties prefer that I use only God's Law, especially in confronting their opponents to straighten them out! I affirm that God's Law is important in working with disputing parties, especially when dealing with unrepentance. In turning people's attention to Christ, we need to distinguish and apply both Law and Gospel. For many, guiding people according to God's Word has often led to the use of the Law to the exclusion of the Gospel. The assumption of well-meaning believers is that Christians already *know* the Good News about salvation through Jesus and therefore no longer need its power. Nothing could be farther from the truth. The Gospel provides the power that turns stubborn hearts toward God in repentance and confession. This is not a "once-in-a-lifetime" event; it is an ongoing, daily work of God in our lives.

Edward Welch reminds us that both God's commands and His grace work together for instructing His children: "Scripture never expects us to hear God's commands *to* us in isolation from the serious contemplation of God's work *for* us in Christ" (p. 217).

Walther contradicts those who claim that either one or the other is all that is needed: "No, both are equally necessary. Without the Law the Gospel is not understood; without the Gospel the Law benefits us nothing" (p. 6).

Walther warns against applying only Gospel:

> Now, lest the preaching of the Gospel only produce lazy, frigid Christians, who imagine that they need not do good works, the Law says to the Old Adam: Sin not; be godly; shun that, do this, etc. But when the conscience feels these smitings and realizes that the Law is not a mere cipher, man becomes terror-stricken. Then you must hear the teaching of the Gospel because you have sinned. (P. 24)

St. Paul instructed Timothy:

> We know that the law is good if one uses it properly. We also know that law is made not for the righteous but for lawbreakers and rebels, the ungodly and sinful, the unholy and irreligious; for those who kill their fathers or mothers, for murderers, for adulterers and perverts, for slave traders and liars and perjurers—and for whatever else is contrary to the sound doctrine. (1 Timothy 1:8–10)

Commenting on this text, Walther elaborates:

> To all persons of this description, then, the Law *only* is to be preached, and they are not to have a drop of Gospel. As long as a person is at ease in his sins, as long as he is unwilling to quit some particular sin, so long only the Law, which curses and condemns him, is to be preached to him. (P. 17)

Nevertheless, Walther adds this exhortation:

However, the moment he becomes frightened at his condition, the Gospel is to be promptly administered to him; for from that moment on he no longer can be classified with secure sinners. Accordingly, while the devil holds you in a *single* sin, you are not yet a proper subject for the Gospel to operate upon; only the Law must be preached to you. (P. 17)

While biblical commands, laws, and principles are important in helping us recognize our sinful state, the Law does not motivate us to repent, confess, or change our hearts toward God. In fact, Paul reminds us that the Law tends to stimulate us to sin even more: "For when we were controlled by the sinful nature, the sinful passions aroused by the law were at work in our bodies, so that we bore fruit for death" (Romans 7:5). And in a later verse he states, "But sin, seizing the opportunity afforded by the commandment, produced in me every kind of covetous desire" (v. 8).

While promoting proper use of the Law, Walther identifies its discouraging effects: "The effect of preaching the Law, then, is to increase the lust for sinning" (p. 14). In addition, Walther explains that the Law leads to hopelessness because it does not give us the power to overcome sin: "The Law uncovers to man his sins, but offers him no help to get out of them and thus hurls man into despair" (p. 14). Walther further teaches that the Law cannot comfort the sinner: "It conjures up the terrors of hell, of death, of the wrath of God. But it has not a drop of comfort to offer the sinner" (p. 14).

The Good News about Christ, however, gives us

what the Law cannot give. Instead of increasing our desire to sin, the Gospel leads us to repent and seek God's forgiveness, and it empowers us to keep God's commands. To the Corinthians, Paul declared, "For Christ's love compels us" (2 Corinthians 5:14). St. John tells us that our love for God and others is only possible because of God's love for us: "We love because He first loved us" (1 John 4:19). Paul also describes the effect of the Gospel when he writes, "Or do you show contempt for the riches of His kindness, tolerance and patience, not realizing that God's kindness leads you toward repentance?" (Romans 2:4).

Walther lectured about the contrasting effects of the Gospel:

> In the first place, the Gospel, when demanding faith, offers and gives us faith in that very demand. . . . The second effect of the Gospel is that it does not at all reprove the sinner, but takes all terror, all fear, all anguish, from him and fills him with peace and joy in the Holy Ghost. . . . In the third place, the Gospel does not require anything good that man must furnish: not a good heart, not a good disposition, no improvement of his condition, no godliness, no love either of God or men. It issues no orders, but it changes man. (Pp. 15–16)

To lead God's people in the hard work of reconciliation, we must continually point ourselves and our followers to the Gospel of Christ—not for learning how to lead perfect lives, but to be comforted in forgiveness and empowered to resist and fight against the temptation to sin. Reviewing what God requires of us in His Law is only one part of the process. What the Law declares impossible, the Gospel makes possible. Without Christ, God's commands leave us no hope.

In Christian reconciliation, Christ must remain central. Without Jesus, dispute resolution may direct us to biblical principles for godly living, but it fails to be distinctly Christian. Ambassadors of God's message stay focused on Christ. As the author of Hebrews reminds us:

> Therefore, since we are surrounded by such a great cloud of witnesses, let us throw off everything that hinders and the sin that so easily entangles, and let us run with perseverance the race marked out for us. Let us fix our eyes on Jesus, the author and perfecter of our faith, who for the joy set before Him endured the cross, scorning its shame, and sat down at the right hand of the throne of God. (Hebrews 12:1–2)

5

The Second Distinction: The Responsibility of the Church

Another distinction of Christian reconciliation is marked by the responsibility of the church. For decades, the Christian church has been giving away the ministry of reconciliation. *That's a strong indictment!* you might respond. But consider my statement in light of the following situations.

When a couple is heading toward divorce, church leaders often give up biblical counseling and recommend outside marriage counselors or divorce attorneys. When a dispute arises among adult children over the disposition of a parent's estate, the church usually rationalizes that it is better to stay out of family matters. When one church member sues another in a fight over costs of building a new home, pastors and elders frequently throw up their hands and say, "Oh well, may justice be served and the best man win."

Even worse, distressed pastors, hurting elders, dismissed Christian schoolteachers, and other Christian leaders sometimes resort to manipulation, verbal assault, lawsuits, and even physical violence to get what they want rather than to seek reconciliation with help from fellow believers.

How can I make such strong accusations? As a person who has served the church through Peacemaker Ministries for more than 10 years, I have witnessed countless cases where we encouraged hurting parties to seek help from church leaders, only to see them referred to attorneys or outside counselors with the closing apology, "I'm sorry—there is nothing more I can do."

In many situations people do need professional legal counsel and can benefit from licensed counselors. But too many church leaders quickly wash their hands of serving their members after they refer them to outside professionals. They assume that the church has nothing else to offer. Yet sinners hurting from unresolved conflict are in great need of the church's care, because such people need the healing that comes only from the ministry of reconciliation.

Disputing parties need to understand how their fights and quarrels are driven by their sinful desires (James 4:1–3). They lack comfort from knowing that God provides the answer to their most pressing conflict needs. They seek power to deal with their issues. What they need is forgiveness from God, who then provides strength to overcome their sinful desires and drives them to seek reconciliation. Encouragement springs from the Gospel in knowing that one's sins are forgiven. Lawyers, counselors, and judges may provide important counsel and can help resolve conflict, but they cannot replace what the church can offer in the ministry of reconciliation.

The Church's Role in My Lawsuit

One of my most memorable lessons on the responsibility of the church came through a lawsuit in my own life prior to my work at Peacemaker Ministries. As a personal representative of my father's estate, I leased a commercial property to a man who, I learned, was also a Christian. At once we felt a kindred spirit. However, good feelings turned sour when he neglected to pay his rent. Several times I met personally with my tenant, urging him to pay his rent. I explained that as a fiduciary, I was responsible to the property's three mortgage holders, to some 60 creditors of this complex estate, and to the estate's beneficiaries for prudent management of estate assets. The tenant explained that his business had not yet developed sufficient cash flow, and even after several months he was still unable to pay his rent. Although he repeatedly promised to pay within a couple of weeks, cash flow did not improve and no rent was paid. After months of frustration and unmet expectations, I initiated a lawsuit against the man to have him removed from the property.

My attorneys advised me that my case was solid: my tenant broke our 30-page lease by not paying rent. I could expect justice within a short period of time. I waited 60 days for our court date. The hearing lasted a full day. Then the judge took six months to issue his decision. In the meantime, I paid mortgage payments, real estate taxes, and insurance premiums on an occupied property that produced no revenue for the estate. Although the judge finally awarded in the estate's favor, the war was just beginning.

In spite of the judge's ruling, the tenant still believed he had the right to remain in the property. He intended to pay the rent and was making his own improvements to the property, and therefore he refused to vacate. I responded by returning to court for an order of eviction. My small army of attorneys, sheriffs, and locksmiths physically evicted the lessee and his employees, five other subtenants and their employees, and some 200 storage customers. The subtenants and storage customers had paid their rent to my tenant, but the law required that all be evicted since the estate had not received any payment. People were so angry with me for the eviction that the sheriff would not leave the site until I hired an armed guard to protect the property and until I changed my home phone to an unlisted number.

For the next two weeks, my staff and I met with more than 200 angry people to renegotiate new leases. In the meantime, my former tenant filed an appeal with the court, claiming that I had created a hardship by taking over his business, thus making it impossible for him to pay rent.

Just prior to the next hearing, I received a phone call from Ken Sande, president of Peacemaker Ministries. Ken told me that the evicted tenant approached him for help, and he wondered if the two of us would be willing to meet with Christian mediators to resolve our dispute. Confident of my legal position and indignant that my opponent would suggest "Christian" processes when I felt that he was not acting like a Christian, I refused Ken's help. I rationalized that, as a fiduciary representing scores of secular creditors, I could not subject my legal case to some Christian mediation process.

In spite of confidence in my strong legal defense, the judge ruled in favor of my opponent in the appeal, declaring that I had created a hardship for him by taking over his storage business. Upon receiving the news, I cried out loud to God, "Why is this happening to me? Where's the justice in this?"

Fortunately for the estate, the judge also required the tenant to pay his past-due rent before reassuming control of the property, which he was unable to do. Thus, it seemed, I had won this second court hearing by default. However, I soon found myself being summoned to court for a third round.

I began to count the costs of litigation. In the year this case had ensued, I spent nearly $100,000 in legal and administrative fees, and our fight was far from over. In desperation, I sought advice from Ken Sande. My tenant and I both agreed to Christian mediation.

What resulted was an amazing example of the role of the church in the ministry of reconciliation. Serving on our mediation panel were Sande, the pastor from my church, and an elder from my opponent's church. My pastor was not there to serve as an advocate for my cause. Instead, he was there because I held myself spiritually accountable to him, as the called pastor of my congregation.

As the mediation progressed and our stories unfolded, my pastor helped me see the logs in my own eye, which I could never see before. What were *my* logs? When I was unable to collect rent upon demand, I became angry, and in my anger I sinned. I not only spoke sinful words directly to my Christian brother, but I also "informed" many others about this man's short-comings, expanding on my judgments with the godly intention of protecting others from harm. In reality, I slipped into gossip and slander. Further, when working through a conflict with my Christian brother, I ignored many of Scripture's teachings, and I took my opponent to public court before seeking the help of my church or other believers.

Upon recognizing my sin before my pastor, I con-fessed that I had sinned in my thoughts, words, and actions. Pastor Thompson assured me of the forgiveness that is mine in Christ Jesus, comforting me with the Gospel and encouraging me with the Spirit's power to be reconciled to my brother. My opponent's elder was guiding him in the same way, helping him to recognize his sins of breaking his word, not making rent payment he had committed to, and gossiping against me. We rec-onciled with one another through mutual confession and forgiveness, and then our three mediators helped us negotiate a settlement on the financial matters. In two Saturday meetings we reached reconciliation and settle-ment on a dispute that had evaded resolution in a year of legal proceedings.

My pastor and the other man's elder served us as ambassadors of reconciliation. The leaders of our churches helped us recognize our own faults, and they pointed the way back to Christ for reconciliation. When I sought my attorneys' advice, do you think that they reminded me of Christ and His atonement for my sin? When I stood before the judge in two hearings and in seeking an order of eviction, do you believe that the civil judge warned me about my sinful contributions to the conflict and comforted me with Christ's forgiveness from the cross? No, it was my pastor who brought the healing power of the Gospel to me in the middle of my pain and conflict. The ministry of reconciliation belongs to the church, not civil servants or outside counselors.

Before moving on, let me add that in our theology we follow Luther's understanding of the distinction of the two kingdoms. That is, God deals with the world not directly but indirectly. He does this in two ways. In the kingdom of the right hand, God holds a chalice, a cup of grace. This is His kingdom of grace, the church, through which He administers the forgiveness of sins through the Word of God and the Sacraments. In the kingdom of the left hand, God holds a sword. This is His kingdom of power, the state, through which He administers justice and the punishment of wrongdoing through the laws and force of secular authority. While in this book we are concentrating on the functions of the church, particularly confession and forgiveness, we must not disparage the kingdom of the left. God works through the courts as well as the church.

Whose Job Is It?

Jesus tells us to seek the counsel of Christian brothers or sisters when attempting to reconcile with someone who has sinned against us (Matthew 18:16), and if one or two witnesses of Christ cannot convince the offender (who may also be me!), then the congregation becomes involved (Matthew 18:17).

In his first Letter to the Corinthians, Paul chastises the believers for taking their disputes to court rather than to the body of believers. He shames them for taking their disagreements before unbelievers for settlement when they will be judging angels. He further declares, "The very fact that you have lawsuits among you means you have been completely defeated already. Why not rather be wronged? Why not rather be cheated? Instead, you yourselves cheat and do wrong, and you do this to your brothers" (1 Corinthians 6:7–8).

The church's responsibility to people who struggle with conflict is reinforced in Paul's Letter to the Philippians. When Paul learned of the intense conflict between two women in Philippi, he exhorted the women in his public letter to the church, pleading with them to agree with each other in the Lord. He did this so that the entire church could be informed as he instructed them to be active supporters in reconciling the women: "Yes, and I ask you, loyal yokefellow, help these women who have contended at my side in the cause of the gospel, along with Clement and the rest of my fellow workers, whose names are in the book of life" (Philippians 4:3).

In other places of Scripture, the members of the body of Christ are assigned specific responsibilities toward one another in peacemaking, beginning with the remembrance of peace that comes from God. "Let the peace of Christ rule in your hearts, since as members of one body you were called to peace. And be thankful. Let the word of Christ dwell in you richly as you teach and admonish one another with all wisdom" (Colossians 3:15–16). James urges us to live reconciled lives through confession and prayer: "Therefore confess your sins to each other and pray for each other so that you may be healed" (James 5:16). To the Ephesians, Paul taught: "Do not let any unwholesome talk come out of your mouths, but only what is helpful for building others up according to their needs, that it may benefit those who listen. . . . Be kind and compassionate to one another, forgiving each other, just as in Christ God forgave you" (Ephesians 4:29–32).

Christ gave His church specific charge in the ministry of reconciliation through the Office of the Keys. Luther's Small Catechism speaks of confession and absolution as exercised by the pastor: "The Office of the Keys is that special authority which Christ has given to His church on earth to forgive the sins of repentant sinners, but to withhold forgiveness from the unrepentant as long as they do not repent" (p. 27). After Jesus' resurrection, He appeared to the disciples who were huddled behind locked doors for fear of the Jews. Jesus blessed them with peace and showed His scars to them. "Again Jesus said, 'Peace be with you! As the Father has sent Me, I am sending you.' And with that He breathed on them and said, 'Receive the Holy Spirit. If you forgive anyone his sins, they are forgiven; if you do not forgive them, they are not forgiven" (John 20:21–23).

Because Scripture teaches that the cause of conflict is rooted in our sinful desires (James 4:1–3), reconciliation among believers *is* the business of the church. In the simplest terms, the ministry of reconciliation is declaring what God has done to reconcile us to Himself in Jesus Christ. Unresolved conflict with others often reflects stubborn hearts that refuse to recognize their own sin and the cure available through forgiveness. The church holds the keys to forgiving sins of repentant believers and withholding forgiveness from those who demonstrate manifest unrepentance. No other organization on earth possesses the privilege and responsibility to proclaim this ministry more than the church herself.

6

The Third Distinction: The Necessity of Biblical Counseling

Another aspect of Christian reconciliation that is unique from other conflict resolution systems is the necessity of biblical counseling. Because Scripture teaches that conflict is either initiated or aggravated by sin, Christians embroiled in conflict need biblical counseling.

As in the story of my lawsuit described earlier, we often forget that God is involved in our conflicts. God so loved the world beset by sinful conflict that He sacrificed His only Son to reconcile sinners to Himself. Christ's blood was shed for the sin that gives rise to our conflicts. When we get caught up in our self-justification, we lose sight of whose we are and what is most important. We usually believe that our dispute is only between two people: me and my opponent. We need reminding of God's role in our conflict.

The World View Versus the Biblical View

The world offers many solutions to resolving conflict. Quite a few of those ideologies begin with some basic premises that result in different approaches to conflict than those of Scripture. Building one's self-esteem has been widely accepted as crucial for one's feeling of self-worth and to empower the individual to meet the challenges of daily struggles. Believing that everyone has some inherently good nature within them, one can learn to overcome life's struggles if he or she can simply appeal to that basic goodness in one's self and other people. Understanding the basic physical and psychological needs of each human being helps justify why each person in a conflict needs to get what he or she may want, giving us insights on how to negotiate settlements that address both parties' needs.

Secular philosophies contain valuable insights about human behavior that can be helpful for all people, including Christians. However, Christians must recognize the fallacies in those ideologies in order to judge their total truthfulness in light of Holy Scripture, or they may be misled into behaviors that contradict their faith and lead them away from godly reconciliation.

While having self-confidence *is* important in both conflict resolution and reconciliation, Christians must be careful *whom* our confidence is in and *through whom* we have value. Scripture teaches that all men have failed to please God in any way. Even our best efforts to do good add nothing to our personal worth. We are precious to God, priceless in our Creator's eyes, because of *whose* we are, not because of who we make ourselves to be.

In Luther's explanation to the Second Article of the Apostles' Creed, we confess that we are worthless on our own but priceless in the blood of Jesus Christ:

I believe that Jesus Christ, true God, begotten of the Father from eternity, and also true man, born of the Virgin Mary, is my Lord, who has redeemed me, a lost and condemned person, purchased and won me from all sins, from death, and from the power of the devil; not with gold or silver, but with His holy, precious blood and with His innocent suffering and death. (P. 14)

By nature, I am lost and condemned, a person with no worth on my own merits. By God's unfathomable grace and mercy, I am priceless, worth the holy, precious blood of God's very Son, who suffered an innocent death to redeem my life.

The Significance of the Biblical View of Self-Worth and Identity

How does this apply to conflict and the need for biblical counseling? When we find ourselves enmeshed in a nasty dispute, God's answer in meeting our needs of image, identity, esteem, strength, and power do not come from deep within ourselves and our own sense of self-worth, but from the very power of God given to us as His children. While secular counseling might direct us to an inner source of strength, the Bible teaches that what we really need is divine power. As St. Peter writes:

His divine power has given us everything we need for life and godliness through our knowledge of Him who called us by His own glory and good-ness. Through these He has given us His very great and precious promises, so that through them you may participate in the divine nature and escape

the corruption in the world caused by evil desires.
(2 Peter 1:3–4)

The evil desires that battle within our hearts as identified in James 4 can be overcome, not with increased
self-actualization, but only with the power of God.
Those who have been adopted by God through Baptism
are promised access to this gift through His very means
of grace.

Some argue that modern approaches to increasing
one's self-confidence do not directly conflict with Scripture but actually help one realize the great person that
God created him to be. But the approach to building
one's perception of self-worth directly contradicts biblical teaching on who we are and what God has done for
us. The promotion of self-esteem and positive self-image
counseling can lead people into dangerous territory,
away from biblical views of their worth in Christ and
the need for their dependence upon God. The more we
seek to make ourselves feel good because of our own
accomplishments, the more we are tempted to self-jus-
tify and self-promote. In some cases, the practice of
increasing our own self-esteem can give rise to sinful
pride, wherein we no longer recognize our sinful condition, thereby reducing our perceived need for God's
grace and mercy.

Instead of seeking to improve our image of self,
Scripture teaches an opposing view. Proverbs proclaims,
"Do not be wise in your own eyes; fear the LORD and
shun evil" (Proverbs 3:7). In Romans we read, "Do not
think of yourself more highly than you ought, but
rather think of yourself with sober judgment, in accor-

dance with the measure of faith God has given you" (Romans 12:3). In Paul's second Letter to Corinth he declares that we should not seek to live for ourselves to our own satisfaction, but to Christ: "One died for all, and therefore all died. And He died for all, that those who live should no longer live for themselves but for Him who died for them and was raised again" (2 Corinthians 5:14–15).

Rather than believing that every person is fundamentally good, Paul reminded the Roman Christians that the Old Testament says just the opposite: "As it is written: There is no one righteous, not even one; there is no one who understands, no one who seeks God. All have turned away, they have together become worthless; there is no one who does good, not even one" (Romans 3:10–12). It's not great self-esteem language, is it?

Edward Welch underscores why it is critical for faith to recognize sin as our key problem in life:

> Notice what happens when we lose sight of these biblical teachings. If sin is not our core problem, the gospel itself—the thing of first importance—is marginalized. The good news that Jesus proclaimed and offered is that there is forgiveness of sins, not through our own attempts to please God, but by placing our confidence in Jesus himself, in his death and resurrection. If sin is not our primary problem, then the gospel of Jesus is no longer the most important event in all of human history. (P. 21)

In the world we are surrounded by great sounding

advice and ideologies for living life at its best and resolving our conflicts. The world's widely accepted philosophies ignore Scripture's fundamental teaching about our sin and our Savior. In order to discern that which is beneficial from worldly sources and avoid the pitfalls of false hopes, we need God's Word to guide us. Scripture points us back to Christ, the Alpha and Omega, who provides everything we need for life and salvation. For Christians in conflict, biblical counseling is a necessity, not an option.

Self-Assurance Leads to Self-Deception

In my experience with conflicted congregations, I have seen the need for biblical counseling. In one case where a congregation split twice over conflicts centering around the pastor, a final appeal hearing was held to determine whether this minister would lose his ordination within his denomination. After being confronted with more than 20 witnesses who testified against him in the hearing, the hearing officer asked the pastor about the testimonies. Over and again, this man justified every word and action he took. The officer questioned the pastor's self-righteous attitude, and the pastor exclaimed with passion, "Look! I know I am a sinner, but I have done nothing wrong!"

In five years of pastoral ministry of a church in turmoil, he believed that he was innocent of any actual sin. Confident in his self-worth, he flaunted his expansive knowledge of doctrine, quoting theologians in Greek and German, proving that he understood exactly how to live and that he had performed his duties perfectly. It was those sinful congregants who needed to be on trial. As he ended his speech, he pointed to the hearing officer and concluded with, "If you uphold the decision to defrock me, you will be sinning against God!"

This man's knowledge about God was so comprehensive that he no longer needed Jesus because he had attained perfection on his own. Modern counseling might help him to understand that he was a little too arrogant or disrespectful to authority, but from a biblical point of view, he was a man in danger of losing his very soul. He confessed a strong faith in his own self-worth. He achieved maximum self-esteem through his own deeds. He could preach Christ crucified with doctrinal purity for sinners who needed it, but he deceived himself in comprehending his own need for Jesus.

Once again, who is most responsible for providing sound biblical counsel when people are in desperate need of the Gospel? Christ's church, the body of believers, has the privilege and calling to serve as ambassadors of the ministry of reconciliation. Biblical counseling is key in reconciling conflict.

7

The Fourth Distinction: The Comprehensiveness of God's Word

For reconciliation founded in Jesus Christ, another distinction is the comprehensiveness of God's Word. Most Christians will readily agree that the Bible is meaningful for bringing people to faith and nurturing our walk with God. But many people overlook Scripture and seek direction from popular self-help sources to solve the intense problems of daily life, assuming that Scripture speaks primarily about eternal matters and doesn't really address modern issues.

God tells us otherwise. He declares that he provides everything we require for life: physically, emotionally, and spiritually. All that is needful begins and ends with our Creator, the Bible's author.

"The fear of the LORD is the beginning of knowledge, but fools despise wisdom and discipline" (Proverbs 1:7). Jesus urged us: "Therefore I tell you, do not worry about your life, what you will eat or drink; or about your body, what you will wear" (Matthew 6:25). He directed us to the source of life for meeting our needs: "For the pagans run after all these things, and your heavenly Father knows that you need them. But seek first His kingdom and His righteousness, and all these things will be given to you as well" (Matthew 6:32–33).

We grow in our knowledge and faith in God through His Word. "All Scripture is God-breathed and is useful for teaching, rebuking, correcting and training in righteousness, so that the man of God may be thoroughly equipped for every good work" (2 Timothy 3:16–17). Through the Word, we receive power to live as children of God. "His divine power has given us everything we need for life and godliness through our knowledge of Him who called us by His own glory and goodness" (2 Peter 1:3). The psalmist also prays, "Your word is a lamp to my feet and a light for my path" (Psalm 119:105).

When wrestling with the challenges of life, we must return to the fundamentals. What drives our passions, our desires, our wants? Paul admonished the Romans, the Corinthians, the Galatians, and us to guard against evil desires that fuel our passion for sin. Sin leads us into conflict, just as it did for first-century Christians. Paul also exhorts Christians: "Be very careful, then, how you live—not as unwise but as wise, making the most of every opportunity, because the days are evil. Therefore do not be foolish, but understand what the Lord's will is" (Ephesians 5:15–16).

From the Playground to the Courtroom

Since God's Word is totally authoritative, its teaching on reconciliation is crucial to all peacemaking efforts. The Bible provides direction for every kind of controversy, ranging from schoolyard brawls to marriage quarrels, church splits, employment disputes, and multimillion dollar lawsuits.

In the legal battle with my tenant, we wrestled over the clauses in a lengthy lease agreement. Our controversy involved matters of real estate occupancy, rights of tenants and landlords, written commitments, state and federal laws, and many other matters. Convinced of my legal position, I resisted help from a fellow believer or my church. I failed to appreciate how Scripture applied to this temporal matter. By segmenting my faith life from my secular life, I lost sight of God's intention to guide me in every aspect of life. I denied any personal wrongdoing and justified my actions. I ignored biblical commands of using fellow believers to help us in reconciling our relationship and resolving our conflict.

It was only after I wasted $100,000 and a full year of fruitless labors that I became discouraged with the world's way of resolving the matter, and I finally conceded to consider God's way. Then, with the help of godly counsel and direction from Scripture, we resolved our battle and reconciled our relationships. God's Word was sufficient and comprehensive.

The world offers many resources that are beneficial. Wise counselors provide behavioral insights. Doctors diagnose medical abnormalities that can be treated with medication. Attorneys guide us in properly understanding and applying law to our situations. Enforcement officers provide protection against those who threaten people and property, and courts promote justice. Other consultants use research and experience to coach us in problem solving.

For the child of God, Scripture is never an option among the many resources available. Inspired by the Creator of all people and all things, the Bible is our primary source for understanding all that is needful for life. In fact, all that is useful for us from the world's resources stems from God and His Word. Wise counsel originates with God's wisdom. The ultimate healer of all diseases is God, who blesses us with medical research and practitioners. Our society's legal system is derived from God's commandments. God established civil authority for providing protection and justice.

Nevertheless, resources available from society are tainted by sin. In contrast, God's Word is holy and unadulterated. Thus, the Bible remains our ultimate resource for working through any difficulty in life. Christians critically evaluate worldly sources to ensure that their approach is consistent with God's will.

At Peacemaker Ministries we have witnessed Scripture's power and application in almost any kind of conflict possible. Past cases include wrongful death suits, various forms of inappropriate sexual behaviors, types of assault by physical violence, embezzlement and other crimes, numerous legal complications, conflicted groups, government leadership battles, cross-cultural and ethnic tensions, and other conflicts. In many of these examples, outside professionals provided key assistance, but Scripture never ceased to be indispensable.

For All Cultures and Times

Because God inspired Scripture for all people, its

truths extend beyond North American borders or the English language. Biblical reconciliation is happening throughout the world and has occurred throughout history, wherever God's people confess and forgive sin. Our ministry's staff experiences this every time we encounter different cultures within this country and from around the globe.

When I first traveled to India for training reconcilers, I was concerned how my teaching on reconciliation would translate. I feared that differences such as poverty, societal influences from Hindu culture, multiple languages reflecting differences in thinking, and other factors might become barriers to the principles of peacemaking. For example, cultural approaches to confrontation and discipline can vary significantly. I wondered if my stories about North Americans in conflict would be as meaningful to people in a radically different environment.

I experienced what I inwardly knew. Biblical teaching is cross-cultural and eternally applicable to people of all times and places. As we worked together in India and learned from one another, it became clear to me that at the core people are people. We are all born in sin. We all contemplate sinful desires that result in sinful words and deeds. We all need a Savior from sin. We all find forgiveness in the cross of Christ. In fact, the Indians especially related to the stories about my and other people's struggles with conflict. Brothers and sisters around the world experience the same pain from sin's effects. Together we celebrate the same reconciliation to God, and all of us can reconcile with other people through confession and forgiveness. Incidentally, I now have a few stories about Indian Christians who reconciled through confession and forgiveness that I use to encourage North Americans too!

Scripture is comprehensive and sufficient for guiding people to reconcile relationships and resolve material issues.

8

Confess Your Sins
to Profess Your Faith

While nonbelievers can apply the basic principles to work through their disputes, the four distinctions described above separate Christian reconciliation from any other process in the world. The centrality of Christ, the responsibility of the church, the necessity of biblical counseling, and the comprehensiveness of Scripture make the ministry of reconciliation unique and powerful because it is founded on God's work for us in Christ Jesus.

Ambassadors of reconciliation profess our faith in Christ when we confess our sins and forgive the sins of others in Christ. The reverse is also true. Our witness to Christ suffers miserably when we justify ourselves or refuse to forgive others who sin against us.

In John's first Epistle he writes about this: "If we claim to be without sin, we deceive ourselves and the truth is not in us. If we confess our sins, [God] is faithful and just and will forgive us our sins and purify us from all unrighteousness. If we claim we have not sinned, we make Him out to be a liar and His word has no place in our lives" (1 John 1:8–10).

Whom do we really fool if we deny our sin? If I claim to be righteous on my own merit, I can fool God, right? *Preposterous!* Perhaps if I prove my innocence to my opponent, she can be outwitted! *Ridiculous!* When I tell my spouse and children my side of the story, they will see how righteous I am! *Really?* Well, at least the other members of my church family know what a good Christian I am, and they will support my innocence in all my conflicts! *Who am I really kidding?*

Scripture identifies whom we deceive when we claim to be without sin: *ourselves!* But the most terrifying words of 1 John 1:8 are in the next few words (emphasis added): "and the *truth* is not in us." Jesus tells us, "I am the way and the *truth* and the life" (John 14:6, emphasis added). When we deny the truth about our own sin, whether original sin or actual sin, we deny our need for Christ. Those who are righteous by themselves have no need of a Savior.

When we justify ourselves instead of admitting our sins, in effect we are saying: "Jesus, I don't need You any longer. *I have arrived!* I was baptized in the church. I was confirmed at the altar. I sang in the choir. I served on the ladies' guild. I was elected president of my church. I graduated from Concordia University! I have a divine call! You know, Lord, I have become the perfect Christian, and I no longer commit sin—at least not in this conflict. Thanks for Your offer, but Your blood and righteousness are not necessary for me today."

Deny our sin, and we deny our faith in a Savior from sin. Thanks be to God that we need not flounder in this hell-bound stupor. We find the perfect cure for our sinful condition in the words of verse 9: "If we confess our sins, [God] is faithful and just and will forgive us our sins and purify us from all unrighteousness."

Righteousness is ours! We are proven justified before God! We are members of the *holy* Christian church. Forgiveness through the blood of Christ cleanses us from all sin, and we stand before the almighty God as blameless. We receive this precious gift when we acknowledge who we are without Christ (sinful creatures), what we have done on our own merit (failed miserably), and what God has made us through His Son (holy saints). In repentance and confession of sin, we profess our faith in Christ.

The word *confess* literally means "say the same as." When I confess my sins, I repeat what God declares: I am a sinner by birth, I sin daily, and I deserve nothing but God's wrath and punishment. When I confess my faith in the words of the Apostles' Creed, I acknowledge what God teaches in the Bible: He created me, He redeemed me, and He sanctified me.

When we confess our sins to God and to others, we also confess our need for Christ. Essentially, our confession of sin demonstrates our profession of faith.

Confession of Sin Proclaims Christ

In filling a position at Peacemaker Ministries, I interviewed Chris, a young man from our congregation. Because our work often requires us to share our faith with others, I asked Chris about his walk with God. He told me that he sometimes struggled in his faith, but through prayer and Bible study Chris found strength to overcome times of doubt. He then gave me an example of what he meant.

As a high school senior, Chris registered for three classes to meet requirements for graduation. Two classes were set by statute, but the third was one of Chris's choosing. Because Chris loved to spend time working out, he selected a work-study program in the gym. To receive credit, he simply needed to complete several tasks in the gymnasium during the assigned class time. No teacher would be present. The student logged his own time based on an honor system.

At first Chris followed procedures closely. A few other students enrolled for the same period, and if they finished their duties early, they would lift a few weights or shoot some hoops.

Over time, however, the boys would slack off from performing their duties and just goof off. After all, they reasoned, no one really seemed to notice. As long as they completed their logs, they would receive full credit. Chris told me that some days he didn't even bother to show up, since he knew he could get away with it. He even neglected to keep up his log.

In the week before the semester's end, Chris began to fill in the blank spaces in his log as if he had showed up and worked. But suddenly he stopped himself. "Chris, what are you doing? You're a child of God. This is wrong because it's a lie." Chris shuddered as he considered the consequences of being honest. He needed the credits to graduate. What would his teacher say? Or his friends? Or his parents?

Chris struggled for the next several days as he considered his options. He prayed for God's help, admitting his sin but knowing that he needed to do more. He pleaded that God would help him get through this mess, even though Chris knew that it was purely his own doing. He still was unsure how he would handle the truth when he went to see Mr. Thomas to present his log for credit.

"Hi, Chris. Let me see your log."

"I'm sorry, but I can't show it to you, Mr. Thomas, because it's a lie."

"What?!"

"Well, Mr. Thomas, the truth is that I didn't always show up for class. At first I did all my work. But later I figured that as long as I filled out my log, I didn't really have to show up all the time. No one checked to see whether I worked or not, so I goofed off a lot when I did go, and sometimes I just skipped class. I even got lazy about keeping my log current. So, last week I was filling in all the days that I really didn't work, and I stopped myself. You see, Mr. Thomas, I'm a Christian. And what I was doing was wrong in the eyes of God. I have to be honest with you. I didn't complete my work. I don't deserve credit. Please give me an F."

"What? Why are you telling me this?"

"I told you, Mr. Thomas. I'm a Christian. That's why. Let me tell you what Jesus means to me."

Chris then shared his faith with his public high school teacher, right there in the school office. A tear rolled down Mr. Thomas's cheek, and he shook his head.

"I've never met a student like you before, Chris. You're right. You didn't complete the work assigned. But you have an integrity that I've never seen in any other student. Even though you deserve an F because you didn't do the work, you've learned something much more valuable than this study program intended. Because of your growth in character, I'm giving you a passing grade anyway."

As Chris relayed his story, he expressed disappointment that Mr. Thomas did not acknowledge any faith in Christ after Chris shared the Gospel with him. But Chris also told me he continues to pray for him, asking God to bring him to faith or increase his faith in Jesus.

Notice what happened when Chris admitted his sin. He confessed his sin to God, knowing that he was a forgiven child of God. He received strength and power from Christ's forgiveness to do what was right before God, in spite of the possible consequences. When Chris admitted wrongs to his teacher in a secular setting, he also professed his faith in Jesus Christ. Confession of sin proves our faith in the One whose blood sets us free. Compelled by Christ's love, Chris's focus on his own problems lessened as he became concerned about his teacher's spiritual condition. What an ambassador of reconciliation!

Self-Righteous Defenses Deny Christ

As a contrast, I worked with a congregation where the pastor resigned in frustration over the conflicts in the church. In meetings with the lay leadership I reinforced the importance to work toward reconciliation in order to bring healing for the congregation as well as for the pastor and his family. If a professional church worker leaves a church without making every attempt to reconcile, the church worker takes the pain of his unreconciled conflict into his next congregation. Likewise, the former congregation frequently carries the baggage of their unreconciled controversy into the relationship with an unsuspecting new church worker. Mistrust and suspicion born in unreconciled conflict expect the worse and usually find it.

The pastor agreed to talk briefly with me, but he refused to meet in the church. "I shook the dust off of my feet when I left that place!" He denied that he needed to reconcile with the people. He explained that he really had not done anything wrong himself, and he patronized me with, "I have forgiven them in my heart. I just don't want to have anything to do with them again." Besides, it would be too painful for his wife and children. He had already found other employment, and his schedule just would not allow for it.

Although he was polite, he pointed out to me how those people really didn't appreciate pure doctrine. With carefully selected words, his message was clear. "I need a church that respects my authority and gifts as a pastor and values my correct understanding of Scripture."

Within a few months, this pastor was called to serve another church that was reputed to be solidly conservative and in complete agreement with his positions. He explained to the new church members that his personality just didn't fit with his former parish because of their liberal leadership, and he assured the new congregation that he was excited to serve them. In less than one year, he became embroiled in several bitter disputes with the new congregants, and he even initiated a lawsuit against them for the injustices he claimed he suffered from their mistreatment. For the fourth time in 11 years, he resigned as pastor.

This pastor dogmatically defended the theology of the church. More accurately, he defended *his* personal understanding of doctrine, and he underscored how his opponents were inept. Because he convinced himself that he was guarding God's truth, he viewed himself as an innocent martyr. As I listened carefully to him, he was able to properly articulate God's teachings. But when it came to applying those truths in his life, there was little connection. He made himself righteous in his own merits, and his words and actions testified to self-justification. He claimed to be without sin. He denied any wrongdoing and, in so doing, denied any present need for Christ. St. John would say that this man made God out to be a liar, and God's Word had no place in his life. For whom was this man an ambassador?

One way or the other, the confidence for the source of our righteousness is revealed in our confession or lack of it. This is expressed in our worship as well. With the hymnist we confess:

Salvation unto us has come
By God's free grace and favor;
Good works cannot avert our doom,
They help and save us never.
Faith looks to Jesus Christ alone,
Who did for all the world atone;
He is our one redeemer.
(*Lutheran Worship* 355, st. 1)

9

Remaining Approachable

Our effectiveness as ambassadors of reconciliation is greatly affected by how approachable we are perceived to be by others. Individuals who suffer from guilt or who cannot see their own sin seek help from those whom they trust. None of us desires to have our ugly side exposed, and we resist revealing our private struggles over sin with people we distrust.

The human need for finding someone approachable in confession and forgiveness is sometimes better recognized by the world than by believers. Some people pay professional fees to discuss their hidden sins with psychologists and other counselors who abide by professional codes of confidentiality. Internet Web sites offer opportunities for relieving guilty consciences in total anonymity. There are even 900 numbers one can dial (for a per minute fee) to make private confession over the phone to someone you've never met. In each of these situations people openly share their private weaknesses because they believe that their innermost thoughts are safe.

Honesty about sin creates shame, and our natural reaction is to protect ourselves by covering up. In Genesis we learn about man's first experiences of shame:

> Then the eyes of both of them were opened, and they realized they were naked; so they sewed fig leaves together and made coverings for themselves. Then the man and his wife heard the sound of the LORD God as He was walking in the garden in the cool of the day, and they hid from the LORD God among the trees of the garden. But the LORD God called to the man, "Where are you?" He answered, "I heard You in the garden, and I was afraid because I was naked; so I hid." (Genesis 3:7–10)

To confront our sin, we must be uncovered. Our hidden thoughts and our "secret" words and actions need to be exposed. In reality, God always knows our sin. It is we who deceive ourselves into thinking we can hide it from God and others. But in order to see the truth ourselves, we often need to bare our soul to someone else.

To whom do I choose to reveal my most intimate thoughts, hurts, weaknesses, and sins? Someone I trust will keep our conversations confidential. Someone I believe will love me anyway. Someone I feel will be able to understand my struggles. Someone I have confidence will comfort me and gently guide me. Someone I admire not only for her biblical knowledge but also for the way in which she applies biblical truth to life. In short, it must be someone who for me is approachable.

Unapproachable Leaders

Think of someone in your life who has been in authority over you. What made that person difficult for you to approach?

We often respect those who have authority over us because they have the power to make life a little more pleasant or to administer consequences. Appropriately, we may hold a healthy fear for them as those who represent authority in our lives. God expects us to respect, honor, and obey those He has placed in authority over us. Their very position produces a barrier that makes them less approachable because of the authority they hold over us. Some people misuse the influence or power that comes with authority, thereby making themselves more difficult to approach.

When I was a young man seeking my first business line of credit, I remember waiting for 20 minutes after my appointment in a professional but sterile bank lobby to meet the commercial loan officer. The secretary finally informed me that I could see Mr. Powell, and she led me into his inner chamber at the back of the department. Arising from a stately leather-bound, high-backed chair, this tall figure in a dark, three-piece suit stood to greet me, reaching out to shake my hand across a massive dark oak desk with an impeccable glass top. He curtly introduced himself and gave a short nod to his secretary, directing her to leave. Responding to the motion of his arm, I seated myself across from him in an uncomfortable low chair with no arms. There was no mistaking who was king in this room.

He paged through my file, half-reclining in his chair as I spoke. Occasionally he looked at me over top of his reading glasses and nodded to indicate that I could continue, but his wrinkled forehead and penetrating eyes communicated that I had an uphill battle. When I answered his question about the amount I was seeking, his face cringed as if I deeply wounded him, and he took his glasses off, sticking the bow in the corner of his mouth. In the long silence that followed, I knew that I had committed a mortal sin. After a deep sigh he stood up to pace back and forth in the office, lecturing me on the dangers of debt. A few days later he approved my line of credit for the full amount I sought, but I always knew what to expect when I entered the hallowed halls of his office. I never perceived this man as easy to approach.

One in authority can easily communicate an attitude of superiority, judgment, and condemnation. Dress, furniture arrangement, gatekeepers, facial expressions, voice inflections, time constraints, lack of eye contact except stern looks, lighting, and other physical attributes can be used to reinforce one's authority or minimize it. For example, in a tense case between a divorcing husband and wife, the husband showed up for the mediation dressed in full military uniform, even though he did not have duty that day. Everyone in the room clearly understood his message: "Stand to attention! I'm the superior officer here!"

Even without positional authority, there are ways to create power imbalances or impress upon others the superiority of your position. People who regularly express anger or disappointment discourage others from seeking their help. Leaders who lack empathy are perceived as uninterested, and those who frequently express disrespect for others are perceived as judgmental and thus unapproachable. Poor listeners communicate that others aren't important. Using intimidating words, condemning others, and putting people down reduce one's ability to be trusted by peers or subordinates. Sarcasm, even when done for comic relief, can easily undermine one's credibility.

One of the greatest hallmarks of an unapproachable person is one who rarely admits his or her own fault or forgives others. What reason would a person have to confess any failure to someone who is defensive or self-justified? Why would someone subject themselves to humiliation and potential punishment by truthfully acknowledging sin to someone who is reputed to be arrogant, indignant, and self-made? How can a person battling guilt approach someone who seems to have never sinned?

Approachable Leaders

Recall people in your life whom you have found easier to approach. Why did you visit with them about intimate matters of your life? How did you anticipate that they would react if you shared something personally shameful about yourself? What prompted you to trust in their integrity?

After I experienced several good years as a real estate broker, our economy nosedived and my income dwindled. Immediately prior to the downturn, I had purchased a newer car for showing homes to clients. Rather than borrow money on a loan with set monthly payments when my income was sporadic, I applied for a personal loan that I intended to pay off in six months from the sale of land I owned. However, the real estate market worsened, and my income dried up. Within a few months, I tapped all my savings and needed the land sale proceeds for living expenses. I stopped by to see Fred, my banker, to renew my overdue car loan.

Fred always left his desk to personally greet me when I walked into the bank. He escorted me back to his desk where we met, but I sat at the side of his medium sized desk, not opposite him. Fred knew I had stopped by to ask for an extension on the note, but he took time to ask about my family. He remembered some of my hobbies, and we chatted for a few minutes about things I liked to do. He brought up the past-due note, but in a way that encouraged me to lay out my current financial woes. Fred reassured me, telling me about a time when he experienced some hard times and how someone gave him some grace when he needed it. He asked about my intentions for working out of my difficulties, but by then he had already given me an extension note to sign. I went through some rough times for a couple of years, but I always felt comfortable talking to Fred and seeking his help for my finances.

Fred was approachable for me. He never used his position as my loan officer to put me down or make me feel more ashamed than I already was. Instead, he encouraged me by treating me like one of his best customers. He took time to ask about my personal life, not to pry but to demonstrate care for me. Fred trusted me, even when I felt that I had not lived up to his or my expectations.

One of the things that I appreciated most about Fred was his transparency. He didn't reveal unnecessary details of his personal struggles, but his admission of imperfection increased my admiration of him and my trust in him. This was a man to whom I could relate. Instead of wanting to avoid him between loan extensions, I found myself drawn to stopping by more frequently just to visit, give him informal updates, and ask for some financial advice.

Do Others Perceive You as Approachable?

We can quickly identify those people who we believe are approachable for us. It is much more difficult to honestly assess whether we ourselves are perceived as approachable by others.

I view myself as easy to approach. I consider myself open and honest about my own faults. I remember all the people I forgive. I reassure myself that I must be approachable because so many people trust me and seek my advice on personal, intimate problems. As a person who regularly coaches people in conflict, I have heard countless heartfelt confessions where I have comforted the guilty with the promise of the Gospel. My conclusion? Ted is very approachable!

More than once I have been completely caught off guard in this respect. Without realizing what I have done, I have, at times, made myself quite unapproachable. I have been unapproachable to people I counseled, to some of my closest work associates, to some members of my church, and even to my family members. Each time when someone has tried to point this out to me, my immediate reaction was defensive. "Of course, I'm approachable! Don't you know how many people share their sins with me? Have you forgotten how many times I have spoken on this subject? Don't you think I know what makes a person difficult to approach?"

Pride is one of my most cherished sins. It often is my favorite defender. I use my self-assured ego to protect myself from "unwarranted" attacks, and it reinforces my inner strength to win the battles I fight. My pride destroys my approachability for some people.

In a relationship with a fellow church member, I learned that he felt I was unapproachable. He had suffered public embarrassment in our church over a sin that became known to a large circle of friends. I had helped reconcile him to several others, and I actively mediated an agreement between this person and the people he offended. In my mind, I was kind to him, I empathized with him, and I clearly articulated where this person had sinned but was quick to apply the Gospel. I thought I went out of my way to say hi whenever I saw this person at church or other places. As you might have deduced from reading these sentences, I defended myself pretty well with "I" language.

As we actually began to talk about our relationship and his feeling that I was unapproachable, he indicated that I was a spiritual mentor to him. As a layman, I defended myself by reminding him that I was not the pastor. "After all, I am only a lay person, just like you!" While what I said was technically correct, he held me in high esteem. His folly was that he respected me for my spiritual leadership. While I assumed we were peers, he looked up to me in ways I failed to realize. As a result, the words I chose and the actions I used around him impacted him more than I intended.

I could possibly justify the situation by explaining that he simply misunderstood our relationship. Perhaps I could say that he was overly sensitive and unrealistic in his expectations. I could defend myself by stating that I was unaware of how this person respected me. Elements of truth exist in each of these statements.

In his perception, however, I became unapproachable. I assumed a leadership role in coaching this person and mediating the situation. I provided biblical counsel including both Law and Gospel, and he admired my use of Scripture. This man made himself vulnerable to me, and we openly discussed his weaknesses. He trusted me with confidential information about his personal struggles. I became an authority figure to this man, and I overlooked how that affected my communication to him. Instead of seeking to understand our relationship from his point of view, I focused on how *I* understood it.

Authority can be given in two ways. *Positional* authority is conferred by one's position: pastor, employer, mother, husband, governor, and so forth. *Personal* authority is granted to one by those who respect the person. Many of us possess both *positional* and *personal* authority when we serve in a stated position and have earned respect and trust from those who submit themselves to us.

God establishes high expectations for anyone who serves in a position of authority, whether positional or personal. To employers and supervisors: "And masters, treat your slaves in the same way. Do not threaten them, since you know that He who is both their Master and yours is in heaven, and there is no favoritism with Him" (Ephesians 6:9). To parents: "Fathers, do not exasperate your children; instead, bring them up in the training and instruction of the Lord" (Ephesians 6:4). To husbands: "Husbands, love your wives and do not be harsh with them" (Colossians 3:19). To all Christians who serve as ambassadors for Christ: "Submit to one another out of reverence for Christ" (Ephesians 5:21).

To pastors, preachers, and elders: "Now the overseer must be above reproach, the husband of but one wife, temperate, self-controlled, respectable, hospitable, able to teach, not given to drunkenness, not violent but gentle, not quarrelsome, not a lover of money. He must manage his own family well and see that his children obey him with proper respect" (1 Timothy 3:2–4). St. Peter adds: "Be shepherds of God's flock that is under your care, serving as overseers—not because you must, but because you are willing, as God wants you to be; not greedy for money, but eager to serve; not lording it over those entrusted to you, but being examples to the flock" (1 Peter 5:2–3).

Although He is holy, Jesus is approachable. He suffered for our sakes. He freely forgives. He set aside His heavenly glory to assume the humble state of man, so that He could serve sinners.

> Your attitude should be the same as that of Christ Jesus: Who, being in very nature God, did not consider equality with God something to be grasped, but made Himself nothing, taking the very nature of a servant, being made in human likeness. And being found in appearance as a man, He humbled

Himself and became obedient to death—even death on a cross! (Philippians 2:5–8)

Gentle, vulnerable, humble, loving, forgiving—these characteristics describe one who is approachable. Nevertheless, these same attributes are often viewed as weaknesses in our world, and people prefer to follow people who exhibit opposing qualities. We admire those who seem invulnerable. We value strong confidence more accurately identified as personal pride. We prefer following those who seem flawless and nearly perfect. We learn to despise those who admit wrongdoing.

Ambassadors of Christ trust God's method for leadership. They are perceived as approachable people because they demonstrate faithfulness in their knowledge and application of Scripture to their personal lives. They do not seek to be perceived as the perfect leader but point to the One who is. God *is* perfect. He *is* invulnerable, although Christ humbled Himself for our sake. He *is* confident. He has no inherent weaknesses.

Christian leaders cannot serve effectively by pretending to be God. Instead, they must recognize their role as servants. Pastors, teachers, parents, employers, and other earthly authorities represent God and His authority but do not replace it. Ambassadors do not assume all the perfection and prestige of the One they represent.

Known by Their Approachability

A man in my church who continues to inspire me is someone I have known since childhood. As my third-grade Sunday school teacher, Lew (his real name!) often acknowledged his own struggles to live as God commanded. During congregational meetings I have witnessed Lew speak on various issues with clarity and grace, disagreeing without offending. On one occasion Lew mediated a dispute between me and another church leader. I respected his words and felt comfortable discussing my faults because I knew that Lew was honest about his own failings. In adult Bible class, Lew is not afraid to talk about his doubts or fears or his mishandling of past events, even though he serves as an elder of our church. He constantly points back to Christ as his source of strength. Lew is respected as a godly leader, not because he is perfect, but because his faith is revealed in the way he lives.

I have benefited from wonderful pastoral care. The pastors who have comforted me most are those who were approachable. Like my Lord Jesus, I trusted them to gently examine my actions without condemning me. Before I opened my mouth, I knew that forgiveness was a given. I confidently poured out my worst fears because I had a confidant who helped me bear my cross. One reason I found them easy to approach was because of their own transparency.

These gifted church leaders did not use the pulpit or teaching position as their personal confessional. They did not publicly confess their private sins before us every week. But they shared stories about themselves that revealed their sinfulness, so that they could encourage those of us who tend to deny our sin. They were quick to admit wrong in board meetings or in personal interactions, asking for forgiveness. They forgave again and again, even when those who hurt them seemed unworthy.

None of the church leaders I admire are perfect. They all struggle with sin. They all resist forgiving as quickly as God commands. But they exhibit those spiritual gifts of joy, peace, patience, kindness, goodness, faithfulness, gentleness, and self-control. They are not afraid of admitting their weaknesses by giving examples in public or by confessing specific sins to those they have offended. In so doing, they demonstrate faith in a forgiving God.

A New Creation in Christ

Can a church leader overcome a reputation of being unapproachable? In one congregation I worked with, the pastor had detached himself from any personal relationships in the church. He explained that by remaining somewhat aloof, he could avoid the complications that arise from jealousy over people who try to get close to the pastor. Over the years he developed mechanisms to distance himself from any of his members, and many of the people in his church sensed that he was uncaring and would not listen to their concerns.

Maria served as chairman of the youth board, and she had been offended by some of her pastor's actions. I encouraged her to talk directly to him. She predicted that he would give her a cold shoulder. Meeting with him would be fruitless. With some encouragement from Scripture to "go and be reconciled" (Matthew 5:24), she made an appointment. As she anticipated, Pastor

Hansen made things difficult for her by limiting the appointment to a few minutes, meeting in his office and placing her opposite his large desk, and offering answers that seemed patronizing to her. She left in disgust and called me to say, "I told you so." I asked Maria for her permission to personally visit with Pastor Hansen.

After some coaching with Pastor Hansen, however, he began to perceive how his protective behavior actually alienated people in his church. While he viewed himself as caring and loving, he was hurt to learn that many felt he was cold and uncaring. Over time he began to consider the possibility that he had neglected to provide personal, pastoral care to several individuals, especially some of his key leaders. He asked probing questions of self-examination that indicated a change of heart from self-justification to repentance.

In a meeting with his church's leadership, Pastor Hansen read a well-prepared public confession. He did not confess sins of a private nature but admitted those things that were known among that group of people. He included his practice of making people feel uncomfortable by being unavailable and difficult to approach. He specifically mentioned that he had sinned against Maria in this way, citing an example from a church council meeting where he had spoken harshly to her, and he expressed hope that he could seek her personal forgiveness when this group meeting was over.

No one spoke a word as he finished, but you could hear several quiet sniffles. I encouraged the lay leaders to read the familiar words of absolution that Pastor Hansen proclaimed to them every Sunday. Uncomfortable silence turned to tears of joy as people recognized the power of reconciliation. Several personal reconciliations followed the group confession and forgiveness.

Later, Pastor Hansen called Maria to set up another appointment, but this time at a place of her choosing. He set no time limit. He asked for her forgiveness, and she freely offered it. Their second meeting became productive for both of them. Two years later I heard from this woman that Pastor Hansen sometimes is still difficult to reach because of his many responsibilities, but for her and many others he is much more personal and approachable. Reconciliation opened the door for broken relationships to be healed.

Is there hope for those of us who are sometimes difficult to approach? Yes, but only if we truly believe our God is bigger than the sins that led to the problem. Paul reminds us:

> Therefore, if anyone is in Christ, he is a new creation; the old has gone, the new has come! All this is from God, who reconciled us to Himself through Christ and gave us the ministry of reconciliation: that God was reconciling the world to Himself in Christ, not counting men's sins against them. (2 Corinthians 5:17–19)

On our own we cannot overcome the sins that keep us unapproachable, and we cannot outlive the reputations we have created for ourselves. But with Christ we are new creatures. In confession of sin and reception of forgiveness, we are given opportunity to start again every day. Scripture teaches us about this daily walk of faith. "If anyone would come after Me, he must deny himself and take up his cross daily and follow Me" (Luke 9:23). "You were taught, with regard to your former way of life, to put off your old self, which is being corrupted by its deceitful desires; to be made new in the attitude of your minds; and to put on the new self, created to be like God in true righteousness and holiness" (Ephesians 4:22–24).

Imagine how unapproachable Saul was following his conversion on the road to Damascus! He was widely known for his persecution of Christians. Saul's life and reputation were radically transformed through confession of sin and reception of forgiveness. Ananias risked his life to serve Saul as an ambassador of reconciliation. St. Paul, as we know him, spoke often of his sinful human condition. We can relate to a man who declared himself "chief of sinners." We can approach such a saint who personally expresses the daily battles we face:

> I do not understand what I do. For what I want to do I do not do, but what I hate I do. And if I do what I do not want to do, I agree that the law is good. As it is, it is no longer I myself who do it, but it is sin living in me. I know that nothing good lives in me, that is, in my sinful nature. For I have the desire to do what is good, but I cannot carry it out. (Romans 7:15–18)

King David may have become unapproachable in his sins against God, Bathsheba, and Uriah. Certainly he lived a long time in his sin. It seemed that no one would rebuke him until the prophet Nathan came to the king with the Word of the Lord. Then, in repentance and confession, David's peace with God was restored in forgiveness. After tasting again the joy of salvation, he recognized that he became better qualified to lead others, teaching transgressors about God's ways and helping sinners turn back to Him. In Psalm 51, we celebrate new beginnings with David:

> Create in me a pure heart, O God,
> and renew a steadfast spirit within me.
> Do not cast me from Your presence
> or take Your Holy Spirit from me.
> Restore to me the joy of Your salvation
> and grant me a willing spirit, to sustain me.
> Then I will teach transgressors Your ways,
> and sinners will turn back to You. . . .
> The sacrifices of God are a broken spirit;
> a broken and contrite heart,
> O God, You will not despise. (Psalm 51:10–17)

Ambassadors whose lives reflect repentance, confession, and forgiveness increase their effectiveness in serving Christ and others. They not only tell the Good News about Jesus, they live it.

10

Examination of Sin

Because of its use in worship services, corporate confession of sin has become routine for many of us. We readily admit that we are all sinful by nature. We confess that we have sinned by "thought, word, and deed, by what we have done and by what we have left undone" (*Lutheran Worship,* p. 158). And when we recite these familiar words often enough, it is easy to rattle them off without examining our hearts or being disgusted about the ugly truth of our sinful condition.

Examination of personal, actual sin is dirty work. It's especially disquieting if it happens to be *my* sin. Should this happen to be an uncomfortable topic for you, you might consider skipping this chapter. But wait—perhaps you and I are just the folks who need to think a little more about self-examination.

How do you examine your own sin? I mean truthfully. Don't list the pat answers you know so well. How do you actually examine yourself to determine if you have sinned? (Honest answers to this question are good warm-ups for self-examination!)

In presenting seminars on peacemaking, I often ask people how they examine themselves. The first responses include these:

- Ask yourself how you have done.

- Think about it for a while.

- Compare your actions to others.

After some prompting, other answers follow:

- Read the Bible.

- Review the Ten Commandments.

- Pray about it.

Finally, someone will suggest something requiring personal interaction:

- Ask someone else to help you.

Whom?

- Your spouse

- A close friend

- God (in prayer or through Scripture)

- The person with whom you are in conflict (there's a radical thought!)

Do you see any missing possibilities? Is there another way to help examine our sin absent from the list? What about your *pastor?*

"Yeah, sure," people will affirm with quiet nodding. "We should ask our pastor."

If seeking our pastor's help for self-examination is a real possibility, why is it that people rarely think of the pastor? This happens whether I speak to groups of lay people, to mixed audiences of lay and clergy, or even to pastor conferences. For many, pastoral care and counseling no longer equate to applying the Gospel to the guilty conscience in confession and absolution. Thus, we do not practice seeking our pastor's care when troubled by sin or when comfortable in our self-righteous piety.

Is Examination of My Sin Really Necessary?

Why do we not ask for help in self-examination of sin?

Here lies an ironic tragedy of the church. We do not ask our pastor to help examine our sinful hearts because we do not want him to know what sinners we really are. That's right! We want him to see all our good deeds. We want him to know how much we give in offerings. We tell him about the sick people we visited. We report to him the committees on which we labor. We let him hear about all the other good that we have done. Consciously or not, we strive to communicate, "Yep, Pastor, I'm a pretty good Christian if I do say so myself!"

We not only put on a good front for our pastor, but we also pretend we are perfect among the other members of our church. Clergy are sometimes even better at this charade among church members or their peers. Like a doctor who rarely visits his personal physician, pastors often hesitate to discuss personal sins with a brother pastor. Bonhoeffer noted this about congregational interaction:

> The pious fellowship permits no one to be a sinner. So everybody must conceal his sin from himself and from the fellowship. We dare not be sinners. Many Christians are unthinkably horrified when a real sinner is suddenly discovered among the righteous. So we remain alone with our sin, living

in lies and hypocrisy. The fact is that we *are* sinners! (P. 110)

When we suffer from physical ailments, we have little difficulty in telling our doctor all about our hurts and aches, and we freely report intimate details about our lifestyle that may have contributed to our ills. We realize that he must be informed to help diagnose our disease or injury in order to prescribe treatment. Some of us may try to convince him that we exercise or eat balanced meals more than we actually do. But as he checks our weight, listens to our heart, and examines and probes our physical body, our true condition is exposed. Even when we believe we are healthy, we often invite careful examination for regular checkups. We submit ourselves to invasive scrutiny, whether we believe we are healthy or sick, for maintaining our physical health.

Isn't it fascinating how the Christian is more likely to be candid to his physician about intimate physical details than to be transparent with his pastor, who can administer spiritual healing? For the believer, which is more important? Moreover, who provides pastoral care for the pastor?

Jesus teaches us that eternal needs are much more serious than bodily concerns: "I tell you, My friends, do not be afraid of those who kill the body and after that can do no more. But I will show you whom you should fear: Fear Him who, after the killing of the body, has power to throw you into hell. Yes, I tell you, fear Him" (Luke 12:4–5).

Even for the regenerate, the desire to be righteous

on our own tempts us to deny sin. King David spiraled into a pit of denial as he ignored his sins of lust, coveting, misuse of authority, adultery, lies, cover-ups, and murder (2 Samuel 11). Jesus emphasized this danger to His followers: "You hypocrite, first take the plank out of your own eye, and then you will see clearly to remove the speck from your brother's eye" (Matthew 7:5). John wrote to believers, "If we claim to be without sin, we deceive ourselves and the truth is not in us" (1 John 1:8).

In *Dying to Live: The Power of Forgiveness,* Harold Senkbeil describes this common plight of self-made heroes of righteousness:

> It's a simple matter of truth. Left to ourselves, we make excuses for sin. We tell ourselves we had no choice; others were to blame. Sometimes we create a whole fictitious world of our own, rewriting the script of reality. And in that script we're always the starring character. In our view of reality, we're always the hero. The villain is the other guy. (P. 85)

Left to our own vices, we slip into believing that our own sins are not as bad as others. Self-justification leads to a myriad of other sins, not the least of which is judging. Bonhoeffer identifies this trap: "It is the struggle of the natural man for self-justification. He finds it only in comparing himself with others, in condemning and judging others. Self-justification and judging others go together, as justification by grace and serving others go together" (p. 91). Bonhoeffer later concludes, "If my sinfulness appears to me to be in any way smaller or less detestable in comparison with the sins of others, I am still not recognizing my sinfulness at all" (p. 96).

Admitting the repulsiveness of our filthy sin leaves us in desperate need for healing. Confession follows with the anticipation of Good News: *your sins are forgiven—go in peace.*

The Psalter expresses the oppressiveness of unconfessed sin and the freedom found in confession and forgiveness:

When I kept silent,
my bones wasted away
through my groaning all day long.
For day and night
Your hand was heavy upon me;
my strength was sapped
as in the heat of summer.
Then I acknowledged my sin to You
and did not cover up my iniquity.
I said, "I will confess
my transgressions to the LORD"—
and You forgave
the guilt of my sin." (Psalm 32:3-5)

Like examination of our physical bodies, examination of sin can be salutary. We seek medical assistance when we experience pain or discomfort, bodily malfunction, or physical injury. For preventative care, we undergo medical reviews even when there seem to be no symptoms. Diagnosis begins with examination of the symptoms and description of the events that led to the trouble. Tests follow to verify initial findings. The physician administers treatment and recommends changes for improved health.

We should recognize warning signs that indicate it's time for spiritual examination so that we can experience healing through repentance, confession, and forgiveness.

Broken relationships, especially intimate or long-term, are caused or aggravated by sin of all parties. If you have unresolved conflict among relationships of family, friends, or business associates, you may benefit from an examination of your sins. Remember this: the more personal the relationship, the more urgent your need.

If you tend to be critical of others (judging), this is an indication that you may need spiritual examination. If you eagerly listen to gossip and "share" it with others, you are past due for an appointment, especially if you have progressed to defending your actions to anyone who attempts to confront you. St. Paul writes, "You, therefore, have no excuse, you who pass judgment on someone else, for at whatever point you judge the other, you are condemning yourself, because you who pass judgment do the same things" (Romans 2:1).

If you feel fairly confident that you no longer sin much, at least not like *some* people, then it's time for a checkup. Perhaps it's been some time since you had your heart monitored. Don't wait until your heart fails and hatred consumes you—test it!

Examination of my sin drives me to seek personal forgiveness. God loves each of us so much that Jesus would have died only for me if I were the sole sinner on earth. Personalizing and owning my sin allows me to personally experience the joy of salvation found in Jesus Christ. Bonhoeffer observed:

> People usually are satisfied when they make a general confession. But one experiences the utter

perdition and corruption of human nature, in so far as this ever enters into experience at all, when one sees his own specific sins. Self-examination on the basis of all Ten Commandments will therefore be the right preparation for confession. Otherwise it might happen that one could still be a hypocrite even in confessing to a brother and thus miss the good of the confession. (P. 117)

Healthy Methods for Examination

Earlier in this chapter I listed people's various responses to the question on how they examined themselves. Let's look a little more closely at some of them.

Asking yourself how you have done, or contemplating how you have sinned, may be helpful. But for most of us, denial and self-justification quickly disguise the truth about our sin. Comparing our actions to others is especially dangerous because we tend to see others' faults much more easily than our own, and that draws us into judging others. Thus, Jesus admonished us to get the log out of our own eye before attempting to take the speck out of our brother's eye.

Using Scripture, comparing our actions to God's commands, and praying for discernment are much more productive for biblical examination. Inviting a fellow Christian may also prove beneficial. We may ask someone who loves us, such as a spouse or close friend, or we may invite our adversary to assist us in identifying the logs in our eyes. Seeking the counsel of our pastor, as the called minister of our congregation, is also appropriate.

Using Scripture

Scripture cuts away the protective layers of self-justification:

> For the word of God is living and active. Sharper than any double-edged sword, it penetrates even to dividing soul and spirit, joints and marrow; it judges the thoughts and attitudes of the heart. Nothing in all creation is hidden from God's sight. Everything is uncovered and laid bare before the eyes of Him to whom we must give account. (Hebrews 4:12–13)

The Bible reminds us that God finds all people unrighteous: "If You, O LORD, kept a record of sins, O Lord, who could stand?" (Psalm 130:3). "We all, like sheep, have gone astray, each of us has turned to his own way" (Isaiah 53:6). Even the most pious Christian who thinks he has only slightly slipped is convicted in God's Word. "For whoever keeps the whole law and yet stumbles at just one point is guilty of breaking all of it" (James 2:10).

Allowing Scripture to directly examine our hearts is powerful. I was mediating a dispute between two neighbors who were at war with one another over a fence on the boundary line between their properties. As the conflict escalated, Pat had taken his chain saw and decimated part of Al's fence. During the mediation, Al attempted to confront Pat about the attack on his property. Pat became fairly smug about his childish behavior toward Al, and Al lost his temper. Attempting to appeal to Pat's modeling to his children, Al laid a low blow to his neighbor by claiming Pat was a failure as a father. I stopped the discussion to meet separately with the two parties.

In my caucus with Al, I asked him about his choice of words. He was indignant.

"You heard what he did. Imagine what his kids learned about settling disputes with your neighbor. Just go ahead and destroy the other guy's property. What kind of father does he think he is anyway?"

"I know you intended to do a reality check with Pat by reminding him of his role as father. But the words we use and the tone of voice we apply speak volumes about who we are before God. Al, you are a Bible study teacher. I know you highly regard God's Word and depend on it for every aspect of your life. Let's take a moment to review a portion of Scripture. Will you please read aloud Ephesians 4, verses 29 through 32."

Al opened his Bible.

> Do not let any unwholesome talk come out of your mouths, but only what is helpful for building others up according to their needs, that it may benefit those who listen. And do not grieve the Holy Spirit of God, with whom you were sealed for the day of redemption. Get rid of all bitterness, rage and anger, brawling and slander, along with every form of malice. Be kind and compassionate to one another, forgiving each other, just as in Christ God forgave you.

His voice trailed off before finishing the text, and his eyes filled with tears. Repentance replaced his burning anger, and I comforted him with the precious news of God's forgiveness. Renewed in the strength of the

Gospel, Al prepared his confession for his neighbor. When Al confessed his sin of anger and harsh words, Pat's heart softened, leading to his confession, and the two men reconciled.

Using the Ten Commandments

Reviewing God's laws, especially the Ten Commandments, is helpful for examining our hearts and exposing our sin. However, one can quickly glance over the commandments, checking off those he believes he has not broken and conclude, "There now, I have satisfied all of God's commands." In the Gospels, we read about a young man who asked Jesus what he must do to inherit eternal life. Jesus reviewed the commandments with him, to which the man responded, "All these I have kept since I was a boy" (Mark 10:20). How easy it is for us to claim our own righteousness, even before God!

God's commands require perfection of every thought, word, and deed. Examining our hearts according to God's commands includes probing into the condition of our hearts.

When helping one congregation understand the seriousness of its sinful plight, I compared the corporate activities of leaders and members against specific commandments. For example, they sinned against the First Commandment, "You shall have no other gods," when they feared people or things more than God, when they craved the created more than they loved God, and when they trusted their own judgments more than they trusted God. Some of their idols included their favorite worship style, their hallowed school, and their past record of numerical growth. A vast majority of the congregants failed to keep the Sabbath holy because they avoided Bible study. I was amazed how most of their elected lay leaders, even elders, had difficulty in locating the Gospel of John when asked to do so. Unfamiliarity with Scripture revealed their neglect. In my meetings with individuals and boards, people had divulged their utter disgust for one another. I reminded them that they violated God's command to not murder: "Anyone who hates his brother is a murderer, and you know that no murderer has eternal life in him" (1 John 3:15).

When I originally met with congregational leaders, they were confident in their church's achievements and were incredulous that I suggested that some of them may have sinned. They all knew the commands (or more accurately, knew *about* them), but they had not been challenged to carefully examine their corporate life against the meaning of the commandments. Following my detailed examination, my foremost recommendation was "Repent, and believe the Gospel." What followed was a refreshing time of confession and forgiveness that marked a significant change in that church's history.

Using Prayer

Our ancient worship manual, the Psalter, offers several penitential prayers asking for God's assistance in examination. One of the most profound examples is Psalm 139, where the psalmist acknowledges that God knows him intimately, and therefore invites God to examine him. The psalm is an amazing confession of faith when you consider that the sinner asks the holy, omniscient, and eternal God to search his heart and uncover sin. On the other hand, the psalm testifies to the unshakable trust in a God who does not desire the sinner to be condemned but to be restored:

> O LORD, You have searched me
> and You know me.
> You know when I sit and when I rise;
> You perceive my thoughts from afar.
> You discern my going out and my lying down;
> You are familiar with all my ways.
> Before a word is on my tongue
> You know it completely, O LORD. . . .
> Search me, O God, and know my heart;
> test me and know my anxious thoughts.
> See if there is any offensive way in me,
> and lead me in the way everlasting.
> (Psalm 139:1–24)

In prayer we speak to God. Through His written and spoken Word He answers us. He sometimes uses people around us to verbalize His truth.

Using Christian Brothers and Sisters

The Bible encourages us to teach, admonish, and comfort one another, and to share each other's burdens. Members of the body of Christ serve one another as they speak the truth in love about sin and grace. These may be people who are close to us, or it may include those who have something against us.

In Paul's Letter to the church at Colosse we are instructed: "Let the word of Christ dwell in you richly as you teach and admonish one another with all wisdom, and as you sing psalms, hymns and spiritual songs with gratitude in your hearts to God" (Colossians 3:16).

Brothers and sisters hold one another accountable in love for the sake of Christ, not to condemn each other, but to comfort one another with the Gospel and to remind each other about our witness.

To the Ephesians, Paul wrote, "Brothers, if someone is caught in a sin, you who are spiritual should restore him gently. But watch yourself, or you also may be tempted. Carry each other's burdens, and in this way you will fulfill the law of Christ" (Ephesians 6:1–2). Christians bear a responsibility toward those ensnared in sin, whether the one trapped by sin invites assistance or not. Nevertheless, a warning goes with the command to the examiner: be careful that you also do not fall into a similar trap. Examining another's sins can easily lead to judging and self-righteous attitudes.

In Matthew 18, Jesus teaches that the offended person owes it to the offender to show him his fault: "If your brother sins against you, go and show him his fault, just between the two of you. If he listens to you, you have won your brother over" (v. 15). This action may take repeated attempts over a long period of time. Should the offender refuse to listen, Jesus explains that one or two others should be asked to assist. If the sinner refuses to listen to them, then the church carries the responsibility. In each situation, the sinner is guided by fellow believers who help him recognize his sin in order to achieve restoration.

Because examination by others can make us feel uncomfortable, we often resist others' assistance or make it quite painful for them to serve us. If we happen to be in authority, we can make it nearly impossible for those under us to help us examine our sin. In such situations, if we truly desire godly counsel about our sin, we must specifically invite it.

Carol was a lay leader in the church led by Pastor Bock. Their unresolved dispute had caused growing rifts in the congregation by the time I was asked to mediate their case. As we came together, I could see that Pastor Bock was blind to his own contributions to the conflict. I asked to meet with him privately for a few minutes, wondering how I could help him see his sin. Carol was the one who was personally offended, and she was best qualified to show Pastor Bock his fault. However, her pastor's very presence made her shy away, and I knew that she would struggle to say anything helpful without some intervention.

I asked Pastor Bock if he had ever asked Carol for her help in identifying his specific sin.

"What good would that do? Everyone knows exactly what Carol thinks of me. She's been blabbing it all over the church for nine months!"

"That's not what I mean, Pastor Bock. Have you ever given permission for Carol to help you? She properly respects your office, and talking about your offenses to you can be quite intimidating. Would you be willing to invite her to assist you?"

We talked for several minutes. Of course, I reminded him of the grace given him in Christ and whose he was through his Baptism. We prayed for courage and wisdom, and returned to the meeting room. Pastor Bock sighed, leaned forward to gain Carol's attention, and spoke in a soft voice.

"Carol, I know that I hurt you. I thought I understood all the ways in which I did that, but we wouldn't be in this mediation today if you were convinced that I really grasped what you are saying. Will you help me? [He paused to wait until she looked at him.] Will you help me get the log out of my eye so that I can confess my sins to God and to you and seek forgiveness?"

Carol sat speechless. This pastor who seemed so unapproachable to her in the past demonstrated a humility she had not witnessed before. When she finally responded, she spoke in quiet tones, unlike any other time I heard her. Her words became more personal and less attacking. Her pastor asked insightful questions, indicating his careful attention to her words. His eyebrows lifted as her answers provided some keys to comprehending the hurtfulness of his actions. For the first time in months, these two carried on a meaningful conversation. Pastor Bock's self-inviting examination by his opponent became a pivotal event that led to reconciliation with Carol and many others in his congregation.

Bonhoeffer reminds us:

> Reproof is unavoidable. God's Word demands it when a brother falls into open sin. The practice of discipline in the congregation begins in the smallest circles. . . . Nothing can be more cruel than the tenderness that consigns another to his sin. Nothing can be more compassionate than the severe rebuke that calls a brother back from the path of sin. (P. 107)

Using Your Pastor

In the early 1980s I suffered financial struggles as a real estate broker when our market plunged and foreclosures were common. I not only sustained dramatic drops in income, but I also I incurred increasing expenses for marketing and rental property vacancies. I fought back by spending more time working. I reasoned that I could make something happen if I simply worked hard enough.

To stay afloat, I sacrificed time in essentially every other area of my life: family, relaxation, Bible study, devotions, physical care for myself, and so forth. As unpaid bills and past-due notices mounted, I increased time at work but became much less productive. Although losing weight has always been a struggle, I lost 30 pounds in two months, even though I ate somewhat normally. Constantly tired, I tried to sleep eight hours or more a night, only to wake up exhausted from my tossing and turning. Losing hope, I began to wish that God would end my life. That's when I admitted that I was depressed and needed help. I made an appointment with Pastor Thompson.

I had not intended for our meeting to be a time of examination of my sin. I sought consolation and sympathy. Pastor Thompson listened carefully as I poured out my sorrows, and I felt safe with him. But before I knew it, my pastor began examining my spiritual condition. To follow up on my death wish, he asked if I was rejecting the atoning work of Christ for me. *Unbelievable!* I thought to myself. *How dare he question my faith!* Verbally, I assured him that I certainly had not rejected my faith in Christ. The next question seemed just as uncaring. Why had I stopped attending Bible class? *Well*, I thought to myself, *didn't he hear me tell him that I had to spend that time working? Does he have any idea what it's like to be in my situation?* I defended myself by reexplaining my financial woes. Additional questions and comments followed, each given with grace and care. But I didn't seem to notice since my pride was under attack. In my arrogance I denied that I had any doubts about my faith. I halfheartedly admitted to some of my faults, but I also made excuses for others. He took time to encourage me in the Gospel, in spite of my weak repentance, and then he suggested some practical steps to correct my spiritual shortcomings and take more time for myself and my family. We closed in prayer.

As I drove away, my anger swelled in defense of my pride. Then it dawned on me. *Ted, you finally admitted that you were in trouble. You sought help from your pastor because you know he loves you and speaks God's truth to you. You're a fool if you don't put it into practice.*

As I reflected on Pastor Thompson's words, my attitude improved. I remember the evening a few weeks later that his counsel finally took root. It was pleasant outside, and I sat on the front steps of our home, which was currently in mortgage foreclosure. I looked to the heavens and confessed to God that I had attempted to make myself god. I asked for forgiveness, confident in the knowledge that Jesus paid the full penalty for my pride and other sins. My wife came out to see if I was okay. I told her where I had journeyed spiritually. No longer would I sacrifice everything else to make something happen. I committed to her to trust in God for our family's welfare. Even if we lost everything of worldly value, I confessed that a God that could forgive even me would certainly take care of our earthly needs.

Without realizing it at the time, Pastor Thompson examined me. He took the opportunity when the Holy Spirit prompted me to seek his help. To this day, I still resist having my pastor examine me unless I'm desperate. (I don't care for medical exams, either!) Yet, every time I go, I find a shepherd who is there to lovingly apply both Law and Gospel to me in a most personal and wonderful way.

I highly commend using your pastor to help examine your heart.

Using Questions for Examination

Asking the right questions can be quite useful in examination. Whether asking yourself the questions or having someone ask them of you, I find it beneficial to write out the answers. Taking time to write often causes you to be more reflective. Visually, it provides a way to review your thoughts on paper, sometimes leading to further reflection. When counseling someone else, answering insightful questions between sessions serves as a homework assignment that can be later discussed.

In Ken Sande's book *The Peacemaker: A Biblical Guide to Resolving Personal Conflict* he dedicates his fifth chapter to examining yourself. The questions at the end of the chapter have proven effective tools for self-examination, especially when seeking reconciliation in personal relationships. In one of the appendices to this book I have also included questions for examination that were drawn from questions prepared by the Commission on Worship of The Lutheran Church—Missouri Synod. These questions were written to help prepare us for private confession or for the general confession used in worship.

Dangers of Examination

Regular examination of sin can serve as a healthy exercise for the child of God. Nevertheless, abuse of this beneficial discipline can be detrimental, compelling some to live in the despair of perpetual guilt or even leading others to believe that they can gain God's conditional approval for forgiveness.

Examination of sin must not be treated as torture or punishment for sin. Because the reality of our sinfulness creates horror, we must take care to not dwell in that state. Wallowing in guilt does not improve our situation. It can keep us from the life-changing power of our Lord's forgiveness. Ed Welch claims, "Every experienced counselor, secular or Christian, knows that change will not take place under a load of guilt and condemnation. . . . Guilt and change *cannot* coexist. Guilt will stifle any attempt at self-reformation" (pp. 234–5).

Immediately when burdened by guilt, the sinner ought to move to confession, where he hears those comforting words of absolution. A man encumbered with guilt requires relief that only the Gospel can bring. Examining the heart of a guilt-ridden sinner may only serve to depress that person more. Although he may not fully understand his sin or the true depth of it, he needs the assurance that Christ assumed all our guilt on the cross and fully paid for our sins. Those seeking freedom from oppression should refrain from self-inflicted penance or scrutiny by others. When weighed down by guilt, the sinner requires healing through the Gospel.

Sarah carried a massive burden of guilt. She convinced herself that she perpetually disappointed God and people. While her self-declared indictment held elements of truth, Sarah neglected to acknowledge the whole truth including the Good News that Christ had paid for all her sins—past, present, and future. Of course, she blamed a critical mother and an angry husband who piled on more guilt as the years went by. (Notice that even when we wallow in guilt, we still judge others.) When her sin of marital unfaithfulness came to light, Sarah's accumulated burdens became unbearable, and she contemplated suicide. Examination of Sarah's sins was not necessary or healthful to her at this point in time. When one is already distraught over sin, further probing often takes that person deeper into despair. Bleeding people need healing before any more surgery can be done.

In pastoral counseling, Sarah received forgiveness by God through her pastor's announcement of absolution. Even before she really understood the depravity of her sin, the Gospel was administered to give her healing and hope. Further, her pastor personally accompanied her to confess to her husband and to the other man. Provisions were made to ensure that Sarah was never left unattended when distraught. Intentional caring, sharing of her burdens, and regular applying of the Gospel brought hope and encouragement to one who suffered years of depression. Over time her pastor was able to help her understand some of the deeper issues that led to her long-accumulated guilt. Examination of sin in pastoral counseling for Sarah became a long-term process through which she gained new appreciation for the gift of forgiveness.

Another misuse of examination is for self-flagellation. Pious sinners beat themselves with the Law, believing that if they punish themselves enough, they will gain favor with God. They purposely dredge up sins in an exhaustive examination so that every sin may be wiped clean.

In his early years as a monk, Luther struggled with such an attitude as he attempted to please God through various acts of penance rather than believe in the free gift of the Gospel. He rigorously strove to master the piety of religious life through fasting, praying, and even whipping himself unconscious. In daily confession, he mentally tortured himself to identify and confess every sin, wearing out his confessors. One time he confessed for six hours, but soon after became horrified when he realized that he forgot some sins. A weary confessor finally admonished him for rejecting the gift of the cross and trying to achieve his own salvation.

Using examination as a means for punishment is not only an outright abuse of the discipline, but it can also lead to the unholy conclusion that a person can become worthy of forgiveness through works of penance.

Proper examination of sin helps prepare the sinner for receiving forgiveness, but it does not qualify one for being forgiven. Scripture clearly teaches that we are saved by grace through faith, not because of any works, including a detailed and accurate confession of all of our sins: "For it is by grace you have been saved, through faith—and this not from yourselves, it is the gift of God—not by works, so that no one can boast" (Ephesians 2:8–9).

In confession of sin, it is not necessary to enumerate every sin. In fact, it is impossible! Thus, when one is examined, she should not seek to determine all the ways in which she has sinned. Such a process is fruitless.

> Concerning confession [our pastors] teach that an enumeration of sins is not necessary and that consciences should not be burdened with a scrupulous enumeration of all sins because it is impossible to recount all of them. So the psalm testifies, "Who can discern his errors?" Jeremiah also says, "The heart of man is corrupt and inscrutable." But if no sins were forgiven except those which are recounted, our consciences would never find peace, for many sins can neither be perceived nor remembered. (AC XXV 7–10)

Just as we can misuse any gift of God, we must use examination of sin with prudence and care. We ought not neglect the application of this discipline. Neither should we use it to encourage ungodly attitudes.

Examination Is Not the End

Examination of sin is not an end for itself. It is a beginning of a process designed to restore us to God and to others. As reflected in the illustrations above, healthy examination helps us appreciate the depravity of our condition, preparing us to repent and confess and receive the unbelievable Good News that forgiveness is ours.

11

Words That Lead
to Salvation and Life

Richard crossed his arms and blurted the words to his boss:

"All right, Walt. I may have messed up by making fun of you to the guys, but you and I both know that you earned the reputation of a dictator. I apologize if I offended you with my petty jokes, but your grumpy attitude and lousy management makes it impossible for anyone to respect you as a boss. I'm sorry that things have come down to my leaving. You don't have to fire me. I quit!"

Richard may console himself that he apologized to Walt for his inappropriate behavior. But would you classify Richard's statement as a confession of a repentant sinner? Or would you interpret his reaction as more of a defense? Words such as *if* and *but* qualify our apologies and prepare us to shift blame. "I'm sorry I have to suffer consequences" communicates an attitude of self-pity, but falls short of sincere contrition.

Scripture distinguishes between two types of sorrow. "Godly sorrow brings repentance that leads to salvation and leaves no regret, but worldly sorrow brings death" (2 Corinthians 7:10). Godly sorrow expresses itself when we see our offense for what it really is: sin against God and sin against people. Worldly sorrow reveals itself when we appear sorry that we got caught or must suffer some consequence. It is often accompanied by attempts to justify, cover up sin, or accuse others.

Repentance means coming to one's senses and turning back. In the parable of the lost son who squandered his share of his father's estate, Jesus talked about this man's regret: "When he came to his senses, he said . . ." (Luke 15:17). The son returned home to confess, "Father, I have sinned against heaven and against you. I am no longer worthy to be called your son" (v. 21).

The Augsburg Confession (Article XII) defines repentance in two parts:

> Properly speaking, repentance consists of these two parts: one is contrition, that is, terror smiting the conscience with a knowledge of sin, and the other is faith, which is born of the Gospel, or of absolution, believes that sins are forgiven for Christ's sake, comforts the conscience, and delivers it from terror. Then good works, which are the fruit of repentance, are bound to follow. (3–6)

Repentance that "leads to salvation and leaves no regret" is found in confession and forgiveness. Confession of a penitent lays one bare and pitiful before God, open and thirsting for absolution. Faith receives God's forgiveness, which covers one's nakedness, providing comfort and hope, and makes him righteous in God's sight. In response, the forgiven sinner praises God through good works.

Because we are conceived and born in sin, our most natural expression of sorrow leads to death. That which comes naturally is frequently practiced throughout life. Worldly sorrow tends to be on "automatic pilot." Thus, it becomes necessary to choose words carefully for confession of our sin as well as the announcement of God's forgiveness and our personal forgiveness.

Words of Confession

Even when we begin to realize our sin, our practiced words of self-justification and blaming others instinctively fall from our lips. We inherit this trait from our father Adam, whose first confession typifies man's most natural response. "Well, yes, Lord, I did eat some fruit. But it was the woman, whom, incidentally, *You* gave me, that caused me to trip up." Eve learned from her husband's example: "Not me! It was the serpent who tricked me into eating it!"

When we blame others, we really blame God. We call Him a liar. "If we claim we have not sinned, we make Him out to be a liar and His word has no place in our lives" (1 John 1:10).

In addition to examples of lousy confessions, the Bible furnishes us with beautiful confessions, such as David's confession to Nathan (2 Samuel 12:13), and penitential psalms, such as 6, 32, 38, and 51. With fasting, sackcloth, and ashes, Daniel prayed a wonderful confession of repentance and praise for God's mercy, a portion of which follows:

> O Lord, the great and awesome God, who keeps
> His covenant of love with all who love Him and
> obey His commands, we have sinned and done

wrong. We have been wicked and have rebelled; we have turned away from Your commands and laws. We have not listened to Your servants the prophets, who spoke in Your name to our kings, our princes and our fathers, and to all the people of the land.

Lord, You are righteous, but this day we are covered with shame—the men of Judah and people of Jerusalem and all Israel, both near and far, in all the countries where You have scattered us because of our unfaithfulness to You. O LORD, we and our kings, our princes and our fathers are covered with shame because we have sinned against You. The Lord our God is merciful and forgiving, even though we have rebelled against Him. . . .

Therefore the curses and sworn judgments written in the Law of Moses, the servant of God, have been poured out on us, because we have sinned against You. . . .

O Lord, listen! O Lord, forgive! O Lord, hear and act! For Your sake, O my God, do not delay, because Your city and Your people bear Your Name. (Daniel 9:4–19)

Both parts of repentance are expressed in this confession. Contrition for sin is clearly articulated, acknowledging sin before a holy God. Faith in a merciful and forgiving God is explicit in these words. Daniel's prayer testifies to his trust in God by admitting sin and seeking forgiveness.

Specific sins are identified, although he does not

detail an exhaustive list of sins. There is no blaming God or others for sin. Daniel recognizes that consequences are deserved because of Israel's unfaithfulness to God. Praise for God and His mighty acts become part of the overall confession of sin and faith.

Ken Sande summarized biblical guidelines for expressing repentance in confession in *The Peacemaker: A Biblical Guide to Resolving Personal Conflict*. He packaged them in an easily recalled format called the "Seven A's of Confession" (pp. 109–17). I briefly review them here for your reference, but I encourage you to use Sande's book, where he also provides questions to help you construct a confession applying these principles.

1. Address everyone involved.

Often we assume that our sin has affected me and one other person. This ignores the reality that all sins against people are also sins against God. Moreover, our offenses hurt more people than we think. The call to address everyone involved reminds us to carefully consider others who have been wronged by our actions. For example, when I yell at my son instead of disciplining him in a caring way, I usually hurt my wife at the same time. My sin offends God, my son, and my wife.

2. Avoid if, but, and maybe.

Words such as *if, but,* and *maybe* not only weaken a confession, they tend to say just the opposite. Like magic erasers, these words wipe away the words that precede them so that the speaker can direct blame elsewhere. "I'm sorry *if* I offended you" really means "I'm only sorry if it can be actually proved that what I did caused you any difficulty, but it is probably more your fault than mine." What often follows clinches the blame shifting: "but I wouldn't have yelled at you if you hadn't called me stupid!" I justify my slight slip by pointing to your major transgression. Scripture teaches otherwise: "Make sure that nobody pays back wrong for wrong, but always try to be kind to each other and to everyone else" (1 Thessalonians 5:15).

3. Admit specifically.

As in the sample confession by Daniel, identifying specific sins communicates to the other person that we understand how we sinned. "Oh, all right! I guess I made a poor judgment!" and "Everyone makes mistakes" tend to suggest that the person either does not appreciate the seriousness of the offense or is attempting to appease the offended and pretend that nothing significant happened. There is little misunderstanding in these words: "I was wrong. I sinned against God and against you when I . . ." As with Daniel's confession, every detail is not required. Nevertheless, as the penitent conveys sorrow over specific sins of motive, word, and action, the hearer is more likely to sense the sinner's contrition.

4. Apologize.

Webster offers two opposing definitions for *apology*: "1. a formal justification or defense," or, "2. an admission of error or discourtesy accompanied by an expression of regret." In biblical confession of sin, we are obviously referring to his second definition. The guilty expresses sorrow through his apology, "I'm sorry that . . ." Whether the confession is heard as a defense or as an admission of guilt is directly related to whether the person expresses worldly sorrow (justification or defense) or godly sorrow (an admission of sin).

5. Accept the consequences.

Although the believer trusts that the consequence of eternal separation from God is wiped away through forgiveness, he also realizes that earthly consequences may follow sin. When one acknowledges that consequences are deserved and he is willing to sustain them, repentance is obvious. As the lost son returned home to his father, he declared, "I am no longer worthy to be called your son" (Luke 15:21). These words were not a ploy to gain more sympathy, but were expressions of a broken and contrite heart.

6. Alter your behavior.

The granting of forgiveness does not wait for the proof of changed behavior. Nevertheless, a person who promises to amend his sinful ways assumes responsibility for past trespasses and changing future behavior. In confessing adultery to his wife, one man made several commitments to change, such as calling her twice a day when he traveled out of town on business to hold himself accountable. He wrote out his pledge to her, which communicated a sincere admission of guilt and a desire to change. His promises to change helped make his confession credible, which eventually led to reconciliation.

7. Ask for forgiveness and allow time.

Asking for forgiveness requires humility. The request itself is an admission of sin. Forgiveness is God's remedy for sin. From God, forgiveness is granted instantaneously, but from people, it often requires time. Thus, the repentant heart humbly asks for what he does not deserve, and waits on the Lord to help deliver the other person from the dangers of bitterness and unforgiveness. One who demands forgiveness or expects it from the injured loses credence in his contrition.

The "Seven A's of Confession" have assisted thousands of people to express words of confession that leave no regret. However, as with many gifts of God, we can manipulate these principles to achieve ulterior motives. Using these guidelines as a formula for success in order to get someone off your back fails to serve anyone well. In addition, overuse of the same phrases can become a casual ritual that is as meaningless as a token apology.

Words of Forgiveness

Luther reminds us that confession has two parts: first, that we confess our sins, and second, that we receive absolution, that is forgiveness of sins. Psalm 32 reflects both parts of confession: "I said, 'I will confess my transgressions to the LORD'—and You forgave the guilt of my sin" (Psalm 32:5). David's personal account of the two parts of confession is recorded in 2 Samuel 12: "Then David said to Nathan, 'I have sinned against the LORD.' Nathan replied, 'The LORD has taken away your sin. You are not going to die'" (v. 13).

For a sinner to confess his sins and not hear the assurance of God's forgiveness is to leave him in a hopeless state of despair. No other word can comfort the guilty conscience. No other counsel can give power for the penitent to amend his sinful life. No other response leads to salvation and life.

When a repentant believer confesses in solitude, he must console himself through Scripture and faith that his sins are forgiven by God. When another believer hears a brother's admission of sin, that believer fulfills his vocation as ambassador of reconciliation when he declares that God has forgiven his brother's sins for the sake of Jesus Christ. When the pastor listens to a parishioner's confession, he speaks God's forgiveness because of Jesus' blood and righteousness.

Only one hearer of the confession can determine for certain whether or not the penitent is truly repentant. God alone sees into another person's heart. The rest of us must use care not to withhold the announcement of God's forgiveness when a sinner repents and confesses. His confession may be weak. It may have holes. It may lack conviction. But who of us sinners can honestly declare that our repentance and confession are complete and perfect before God? Thus, the Good News in Jesus Christ must be proclaimed to one who confesses.

Since the Gospel itself brings about repentance, we encourage a struggling penitent by reminding him about the grace of God in Christ. Paul writes, "Or do you show contempt for the riches of His kindness, tolerance and patience, not realizing that God's kindness leads you toward repentance?" (Romans 2:4). Sharing the Good News about our Savior empowers us for living the Christian life, including repentance and confession.

Christians sometimes overlook the opportunity to

proclaim God's forgiveness or find it difficult to follow through because of their disgust at their brother's shameful act. But the most significant challenge is announcing personal forgiveness for the person who injured me.

Just as our human nature prompts us to weasel out of admission of sin in confession, that same old Adam prods us to play an angry, merciless "god" when we ought to forgive. Unlike the Lord, who "is compassionate and gracious, slow to anger, abounding in love" (Psalm 103:8), we become indignant and harsh, we fuel our anger and hold grudges, and we stir up hatred in our heart and commit murder (1 John 3:15). We punish the offender by withholding mercy. Or we demand guarantees as a condition of our forgiveness. Sometimes we torture our aggressor by bringing up past transgressions that we so "graciously" forgave before. Without realizing what we are doing, we transform into condescending, judgmental gods who resemble the false gods idolized in other religions instead of imitating the true God, who freely forgives us.

In counseling, one man complained to his pastor, "Whenever my wife and I fight, she gets historical." His pastor corrected him, "Don't you mean *hysterical?*" "No, I mean *historical.* She brings everything up from the past and throws it in my face!"

Where would you and I be if every time we confessed our sins before God, He would stop us and say, "Just a minute, Friend. Let's review the record, starting with the year you were born . . ." God certainly treats us differently!

Sometimes we declare, "I won't forgive until I forget!" What if God said He couldn't forgive us until He forgets? That just wouldn't work! When God promises, "I will forgive their wickedness and will remember their sins no more" (Jeremiah 31:34), it isn't because He is getting old and suffers from dementia! God *chooses* not to remember. He makes a decision to forgive.

Then there's the pastor who complained to me about his previous congregation, from which he recently resigned. "I've forgiven them. I just don't want to have anything to do with them. I will never set foot in that accursed building again!" Picture our plight if God asserted, "I forgive you, but I never want to have anything to do with you again. Go in peace, but don't come back!"

So, a few thoughts about forgiving others may be appropriate.

To help us forgive as God forgives us (Colossians 3:13), Sande recounts four promises of God's forgiveness (*The Peacemaker: A Biblical Guide to Resolving Personal Conflict,* pp. 189–90). When we forgive, we glorify God and comfort our brother by repeating these same promises. In addition, we avoid some of the temptations that lead us away from biblical forgiveness.

- I will not think about this incident.

- I will not bring this incident up again and use it against you.

- I will not talk to others about this incident.

- I will not allow this incident to stand between us or hinder our personal relationship.

These covenants of love imitate the way that God forgives us. Ambassadors of reconciliation represent their God well when they accurately deliver the message assigned to them.

We *know* that we are commanded to forgive as God forgives us, but sometimes it seems impossible. Our reluctance to forgive others is rooted in our inability to grasp the fullness of our own forgiveness in Christ. Peter also struggled with this when he asked Jesus, "Lord, how many times shall I forgive my brother when he sins against me? Up to seven times?" (Matthew 18:21). Peter felt confident that his suggestion reflected a most gracious attitude.

Jesus' answer "seventy-seven times" (v. 22) must have astonished Peter, because it suggested no limitation on the number of times we should forgive. Then, Jesus told the parable of the unmerciful servant, since Peter's query exposed his lack of faith in the expansiveness of God's forgiveness for him (Matthew 18:21–35). While Peter attempted to demonstrate his generosity in forgiving others, Jesus' story pointed back to God's immeasurable grace for him.

Today we disciples also wrestle with granting forgiveness. But we are educated on Peter's question, so we have devised one of our own.

When Should I Forgive?

Once again, the focus seems to be on our benevolence in forgiveness. Our question assumes that we will eventually forgive, but it also infers that we may not forgive for an indeterminate amount of time. Let's turn our eyes to the grantor of our own forgiveness first. Allow me to rephrase the question.

When Did God Forgive You?

When I confessed. When I received His body and blood in the Sacrament. When I was baptized. *Any earlier?* Oh, yes—on Calvary Jesus said, "Father, forgive them" (Luke 23:34) and "It is finished!" (John 19:30). And God's covenant to us was repeated throughout the Old Testament, even going back to the Garden of Eden. In fact, did not God work out our plan of salvation before the foundations of the earth were laid? Paul wrote to Rome:

> You see, at just the right time, when we were still powerless, Christ died for the ungodly. Very rarely will anyone die for a righteous man, though for a good man someone might possibly dare to die. But God demonstrates His own love for us in this: While we were still sinners, Christ died for us. . . . For if, when we were God's enemies, we were reconciled to Him through the death of His Son, how much more, having been reconciled, shall we be saved through His life!" (Romans 5:6–10)

While we were still sinners, even while we were enemies of God, Christ died for us. Notice that our redemption came *before* we were born, *before* we believed in God, and *before* we repented and confessed any sin. God's forgiveness for us came long before we existed.

However, if we believe that Jesus died for the sins of the whole world, as Christ Himself declares in John 3:16, and if sinners were forgiven before they repented or even were born, as we discussed above, then why is not everyone going to heaven? "That's obvious!" you say. "It is because not everyone believes that Jesus died for their sins."

Herein lies a significant insight about forgiveness that clarifies a common misunderstanding of this marvelous gift. The granting of forgiveness is *not* conditional upon repentance, but the receiving of forgiveness *is* conditional upon repentance and faith.

God's forgiveness is available to everyone who believes the message "Repent, and believe the Gospel!" For in our acknowledgement of sin, we confess our need for a Savior and receive the forgiveness that is freely given. Those who refuse to repent seem to think they need no Savior. Those who do not believe that Jesus paid the full penalty for their sin spend eternity in hell, separated from God.

God grants forgiveness freely, without conditions— for we can never earn that which is beyond our reach. God in His mercy brings us to repentance and faith as we meet Him in Word and Sacraments, and we thus receive the benefits of forgiveness. Those who believe that Jesus paid the full penalty for their sin spend eternity in heaven, at one with God.

Now let us return to the original question. *When do I forgive?* If we are to forgive others as God has forgiven us in Christ, then children of God forgive others immediately, before they confess, before they repent. In fact, in order to mirror God's forgiveness for us, a Christian ought to forgive others before they have even sinned against her. *That's impossible—why, that would take an act of God!* Oh. So it would. So it did. Forgiveness is a miracle of God.

We cannot forgive others on our own strength as God forgives us. We are sinners! What inherent right do we have to judge, forgive, or withhold forgiveness from other sinners? Joseph, whose brothers sold him into slavery to be dragged off to a foreign land, suffered many injustices as a direct result of the evil acts of his brothers. Many years later, when Joseph rose to power and met his brothers again, he had the position, and the human right, to execute justice and demand retribution. But he served as a faithful ambassador of reconciliation, proclaiming the wonderful acts of God when he forgave his brothers. He believed withholding forgiveness went beyond his authority: "Am I in the place of God?" (Genesis 50:19).

Since we are all sinners, we have no right on our own to forgive or withhold forgiveness. We can only share that which has been given us. Thus, Paul declares that those reconciled to God are called to share that same reconciliation with others.

> All this is from God, who reconciled us to Himself through Christ and gave us the ministry of reconciliation: that God was reconciling the world to Himself in Christ, not counting men's sins against them. And He has committed to us the message of reconciliation. We are therefore Christ's ambassadors, as though God were making His appeal through us. (2 Corinthians 5:18–20)

Jesus taught His disciples to pray, "Forgive us our debts, as we also have forgiven our debtors" (Matthew 6:12). Jesus warned against those who refuse to forgive others. "For if you forgive men when they sin against you, your heavenly Father will also forgive you. But if you do not forgive men their sins, your Father will not forgive your sins" (Matthew 6:14–15). This does not mean that our forgiveness is conditional upon our benevolent acts of forgiving others, for that would mean that we must perform certain deeds to earn our salvation. Instead, it means that those who refuse to forgive others in essence act like they do not believe in their own forgiveness from God. Those who begin to fathom the immensity of God's gift to them cannot withhold their personal forgiveness for others. Jesus illustrates this point in His parable about the unmerciful servant (Matthew 18:21–35). Our Savior describes a man whose large debt is forgiven by his master, but he shows no mercy to a fellow servant who owes him a debt tiny in comparison. The man who refused to show mercy to a peer ends up losing the mercy given him by his master. Jesus concludes with, "This is how My heavenly Father will treat each of you unless you forgive your brother from your heart" (Matthew 18:35).

When we agonize over forgiving others, Paul urges, "We implore you on Christ's behalf: Be reconciled to God. God made Him who had no sin to be sin for us, so that in Him we might become the righteousness of God" (2 Corinthians 5:20–21). Once again we are directed back to the cross to admit our lack of faith, to confess our desire to put ourself in the place of God, and to seek strength to do that which we cannot do on our own. The apostles connected forgiving others with their own faith when they reacted to Jesus' instruction to repeatedly forgive others: "Increase our faith!" (Luke

17:5).

Jesus, who endured the suffering and injustices caused by our sins, forgives us our sins, heals our hurts, and gives us divine power to forgive. St. Peter assures us, "His divine power has given us everything we need for life and godliness through our knowledge of Him who called us by His own glory and goodness" (2 Peter 1:3). Nevertheless, when we find ourselves deficient in exhibiting the fruit of the spirit, Peter explains, "But if anyone does not have them, he is nearsighted and blind, and has forgotten that he has been cleansed from his past sins" (v. 9).

When offering personal forgiveness, Christ's ambassador recognizes that God is the author and ultimate grantor of forgiveness. "I forgive you, Beth, because God through Christ has forgiven me." We connect our personal forgiveness to God's, praising Him for the ministry of reconciliation. We forgive others *because* God forgives us. We forgive others *as* God forgives us. We forgive others who don't deserve forgiveness *just like* God forgives us who don't deserve it. Attempts to forgive others on our own volition and in our own stead tempt us to play god by serving our own selfish interests and judging others as to their worthiness of our consideration.

"But," you might protest, "what about that scoundrel who refuses to repent? You don't expect me to forgive him, do you?" Again we look to our God for direction. Has He provided forgiveness for that scoundrel? Jesus died for all sinners. Are not you and I the same type of unrepentant scoundrels at times? Forgiveness is offered, whether we repent or not. However, we do not receive the benefits of that forgiveness until we repent and believe the One who gives it.

Now, the redemptive reason for confrontation is made clear. The purpose of confronting the unrepentant sinner is *not* to wait and see if he becomes contrite enough to earn forgiveness. Forgiveness is already a given, and it cannot be merited. The purpose of showing a person his fault is to help prepare him for the forgiveness that is already available. He cannot receive the benefits of forgiveness unless he repents and believes the message. This is true for God's forgiveness as well as personal forgiveness. Those who convince themselves that they have not sinned will not benefit from forgiveness. Those who reject the Good News that Jesus paid for their sins will suffer eternal death.

Therefore, even though we make a decision to forgive, we may first need to prepare the offender to receive the gift. We may wait to announce forgiveness, which is not the same as deciding not to forgive, until repentance. Otherwise, the gift may be shunned, and the sinner remains in his own self-condemned condition. It is not the individual who seeks to forgive the sinner that condemns the unrepentant, but it is the unrepentant heart which brings judgment upon itself. When Jesus instructs the church to treat an unrepentant person like an unbeliever, the purpose of this discipline is to restore the sinner and warn others who may fall into similar sins. This act of retaining sins is not justification for bitterness and unforgiveness, but for saving the lost, protecting others in the church, and giving witness to the world what God commands and promises for us. Those who demonstrate manifest unrepentance deny their need for a Savior, proclaim themselves righteous on their own merits, and thus reject the atoning work of Christ. Such people do not belong to the kingdom of God.

Just like a sick person refuses treatment unless he acknowledges that he needs it, an unrepentant sinner rejects forgiveness because he convinces himself he is without fault. As Walther counsels us, the Law must be preached to the impenitent. And yet, the messenger of God's whole truth must stand ready to administer Gospel upon repentance.

Even so, sometimes we must forgive someone who refuses to repent and receive the forgiveness we so earnestly desire to extend. How painful this is for us, to be sinned against but unable to connect with and be reconciled to the person who has offended us. In a small way, we can identify with Jesus, who prayed for those who were crucifying Him, saying, "Father, forgive them, for they do not know what they are doing" (Luke 23:34). But the reality of living in a sinful world sometimes makes this necessary. With God's grace we can put on Christ, as it were, and from our hearts sincerely forgive someone who has wronged us but now won't have anything to do with us. At least in this way we can bring closure to the episode and move on, and by so doing prevent a root of bitterness from springing up in our hearts.

In preparing ourselves to confront another's sin, then, we must first have made a decision to forgive that person in our heart. When the sinner repents, we comfort him and bring healing through the Good News that Jesus' righteousness covers that sin, because forgiveness is ours together under the cross. Since God does that for us, we can do no other as his ambassadors. Words of confession and forgiveness lead to salvation and life.

12

Professing Faith in Private Confession and Forgiveness

Conflict in a world tainted by sin is inevitable. Every day we breathe, we wrestle with two natures: the sinful nature inherited from Adam and the new creation founded in Christ. In confession and forgiveness, Christians live the Good News and share the Gospel with others.

Jesus commissioned His church to proclaim the ministry of reconciliation: "Be reconciled to God. Repent and believe the Gospel." The Smalcald Articles explain the God-given way of applying the Gospel to sinners:

> God is surpassingly rich in his grace: First, through the spoken word, by which the forgiveness of sin (the peculiar function of the Gospel) is preached to the whole world; second, through Baptism; third, through the holy Sacrament of the Altar; fourth, through the power of keys; and finally, through the mutual conversation and consolation of brethren. (III IV)

Confessing sin is a profession of our faith in Christ, giving witness to our confidence in God's forgiveness.

Forgiving sins of others is the purpose for which Jesus sent us into the world. Confession and forgiveness are daily exercises of faith for Christ's ambassadors.

The opportunities are endless. We frequently miss them because we are not accustomed to recognizing them or practicing the exercises. Thus, illustrations from various settings for reconciliation open our minds to new possibilities.

Mutual Confession and Forgiveness

When two Christians find themselves enmeshed in conflict, invariably they sin against one another. Mutual confession and forgiveness move them toward resolution of their differences and celebrate their common faith in Christ.

Kurt borrowed millions of dollars from Colleen to purchase and develop an exclusive real estate community. Unanticipated delays prevented Kurt from selling lots when planned, and he was unable to deliver his first major annual installment. Kurt and Colleen negotiated an exchange of part of the property, which included a luxury resort home, in lieu of the first payment. However, when Kurt missed his second annual payment, Colleen filed a foreclosure action against him. The two parties directed all conversations through their attorneys, and bitterness and resentment mounted between Christian brother and sister. With some encouragement from their respective church leaders, they agreed to submit their dispute to Christian mediation.

After two days of meetings and hours of laying out hurts and accusations, God's Word moved them to each take the log out of his own eye. Colleen confessed her anger, bitterness, and attempts to avoid talking directly to Kurt. Kurt expressed sorrow over his not keeping commitments, unrealistic risktaking without fully disclosing his financial weaknesses, and blaming Colleen for his wrongs. Both extended forgiveness to one another, and they agreed on a settlement that met both sides' interests. Confession and forgiveness between two Christian business people paved the way for reasonable resolution.

Perhaps one of the most difficult relationships to find healing through mutual forgiveness is between church leaders. Pastors Jamison and O'Brien began a friendship in Christian college as roommates. Years later Pastor Jamison convinced his congregation to call O'Brien as music minister. The congregation flourished in the first few years of their team ministry, but over time unresolved spats led to escalating frustrations. During the rehearsal of the music team prior to the Easter services, Pastors O'Brien and Jamison exchanged heated words in front of 35 witnesses. One week after Easter, O'Brien resigned. Worship attendance plunged as members took sides.

At first O'Brien refused to meet with Jamison and the reconciler. He had accepted a new call 90 miles away and always made excuses to avoid meeting. Jamison blamed O'Brien for not wanting to meet, but he also buried himself in work and neglected to return the reconciler's calls. Finally, the reconciler convinced the two men to meet.

In mediation, deeper hurts and long-term unresolved issues were openly discussed for the first time in their relationship. As ordained ministers, they both believed they were overlooking minor offenses but, in reality, had slipped into denial. Christian leaders often convince themselves they have overlooked offenses (see Proverbs 19:11). But when we neglect to forgive, bitter feelings grow into hatred that exposes itself in hurtful words and actions. Following some coaching from their reconciler, Pastors Jamison and O'Brien acknowledged their sins to one another and confessed them. The room fell silent as their apologies ended. Two men trained and practiced in absolving others forgot to forgive each other. Finally the reconciler stepped in, announcing God's forgiveness to them and then urging them to forgive each other as God forgave them. After granting mutual forgiveness, their faces relaxed and the friendship was renewed. The joint announcement of their reconciliation to the congregation became their most effective sermon on forgiveness.

When hearing each other's confession, ambassadors of reconciliation owe each other the privilege and joy of assuring one another of God's forgiveness in Christ.

What If the Other Person Won't Forgive?

Not every confession of a repentant believer is responded to with forgiveness or mutual confession. Nevertheless, one believer can still remain faithful to God's Word and testify to faith in Jesus.

Tammy shed tears as she admitted her guilt of spending down her grandmother's estate on Tammy's personal expenses while serving as conservator. Emily, the new conservator for their grandmother, labeled

Tammy's actions as reprehensible. Since their grand-mother suffered from Alzheimer's, she was unable to personally respond to Tammy's confession, let alone comprehend the effects of the diminished bank accounts.

Tammy agreed to make restitution, although she had little monthly means and she suffered herself from inoperable cancer. Her confession demonstrated contri-tion, and she vowed to make substantial personal sacri-fices as part of her consequences.

Nevertheless, Emily's personal anger burned against her. Emily could not forgive Tammy on behalf of the grandmother, since that was not her right. But Emily took on a new role, that of judge. She condemned her cousin, seeking ways to vindicate her grandmother's loss.

Tammy realized that her embezzlement also wounded Emily. Without making any excuses for her sin or asking for any release of consequences, she asked for Emily's personal forgiveness. Emily refused. With a condescending attitude, Emily quoted more Bible pas-sages to punish her cousin. Tammy, weakened from recent chemotherapy treatments, collapsed from sheer exhaustion. Emily shook her head, denouncing her cousin's physical condition as simply a way to gain undeserved sympathy.

Tammy never enjoyed hearing words of forgiveness from her cousin. However, her pastor continued to assure her of Jesus' love and forgiveness, and the testi-mony of her faith in that reconciliation evidenced itself throughout the remaining months of her life. Following the death of both Tammy and her grandmother, Emily still suffered from the bitterness she harbored against her cousin.

Private Confession to a Fellow Believer

Confessing one's sins to a fellow Christian can seem terrifying. After all, who wants to admit one's failings before another believer? Won't they look down upon me because of my weak faith? And yet, for some of us, we convince ourselves that we can privately confess our sins to God with more ease than to a brother.

Bonhoeffer confronts this attitude.

> Why is it that it is often easier for us to confess our sins to God than to a brother? God is holy and sinless. He is a just judge of evil and the enemy of all disobedience. But a brother is sinful as we are. He knows from his own experience the dark night of secret sin. Why should we not find it easier to go to a brother than to the holy God? But if we do, we must ask ourselves whether we have not often been deceiving ourselves with our confession of sin to God, whether we have not rather been confessing our sins to ourselves and also granting ourselves absolution. And is not the reason perhaps for our countless relapses and the feebleness of our Christian obedience to be found precisely in the fact that we are living on self-forgiveness and not a real forgiveness? (P. 116)

Fear of man is an idol contrasted with worship of the true God in Proverbs 29:25. "Fear of man will prove to be a snare, but whoever trusts in the LORD is kept safe." When we shy away from confessing our sins to a

Christian brother or sister, we reveal our fear of man and lack of trust in God. Confessing privately to a fellow believer humbles us and proves our fear, love, and trust in God, who provides forgiveness for both the one who confesses and the one who hears.

Great joy and comfort flow from the words of absolution given by a Christian brother. Likewise, the Christian who shares God's forgiveness with a fellow believer also rejoices.

People often ask me if I get tired of working with fighting parties. I don't particularly enjoy conflict, and I do not enjoy dealing with other folks' nasty disputes. However, the greatest satisfaction I receive from being a peacemaker is sharing the Good News about Jesus to those who confess their sins. No other act in the universe is as glorious as God's forgiveness. No other antidote brings such complete healing and peace. The Gospel message we so often take for granted produces miracles of unbelievable portions. And as an ambassador of Christ's peace, I am privileged to watch God working in my heart and the hearts of others.

At first I was uncomfortable with this task. Following my presentations on peacemaking, individuals troubled by their sins would seek me out during breaks and late-night talks. In describing their conflicts, they would divulge their sinful attitudes and behaviors, and ask for advice. Instinctively I knew they needed forgiveness, but I hesitated to absolve them. I assumed that this was solely the responsibility of their pastor and those they sinned against. I reasoned that as believers they already knew about Jesus' love for them. I have grieved over the times I failed to impart comfort that only God's Gospel brings to people in need of God's grace.

Eventually I recognized what was needed. After speaking at one pastors conference, several ministers sought me out to confess their sins, and I asked some questions.

"Isn't there someone else you should be sharing this with? How about your ecclesial supervisor?"

"Are you kidding? If he knew my sins, he could remove me from the ministry!"

"Is there not another neighboring pastor you can talk to?"

"I tried that once [or twice or three times]. I either got stabbed in the back or lectured to for not living the sanctified life of a pastor."

After a few more queries I realized that I was looking for excuses to not declare God's news to the people who sought my counsel. While it may have been true that there were others in their lives that could serve as their personal confessors, I was the person who was hearing their confession at that moment. I personally have experienced the inexpressible joy that one receives when hearing the news of God's forgiveness, and I learned to share it with others who seek relief from their deep felt guilt. What an awesome privilege to serve as an ambassador of God's message of reconciliation!

Recently an elderly pastor approached me following my presentation and asked to meet privately. I recognized him as someone who was highly regarded among his peers. I thought he might want to give me some fatherly advice about my teaching. Instead, he started to speak about a secret sin that troubled him for decades. Once again, God provided me with an opportunity to tell someone about His love through Jesus.

"My brother in Christ, I have very good news for you. Jesus died for your sins, including this particular sin that troubles you. Remember that He shed His blood on Calvary and rose again so that you, too, can share in His victory and live eternally in heaven. Your God now sees you as righteous for the sake of His Son. Your heavenly Father says to you, 'I love you. I forgive you. You are my precious child.' Go in peace, for God has taken away your sin."

I often share tears of joy with a fellow Christian as he hears these familiar words. True, these words are not unfamiliar, but they are precious when given to someone privately and personally.

When a fellow sinner seeks you out to unload a burden of guilt, listen to that person, empathize with that person, and pray with that person. But do not neglect to be an agent of reconciliation. Proclaim God's forgiveness for the sake of Christ. If you are uncertain of what words to use, I suggest turning directly to Scripture. Memorize your favorite quotes of God's grace, or mark several passages that speak God's forgiveness. To help you begin your own list, I have identified a few Bible passages in Appendix C, "Words of Absolution from Scripture." When I have assigned conference participants to share these words with one another, people conveyed thanks for the joy that these words bring, even though they are familiar passages. Apply them first to yourself. Then share the Good News with others. Discover the blessings of your vocation as Jesus' special messenger.

Individual Confession and Absolution from Your Pastor

Totally confident in his sin, Dave lived like nothing was wrong. He fooled himself and others, he thought. But Dave's associates knew that he was living a lie. His pastor came to visit him at his home. Dave was not at all alarmed as his pastor began to share a story with him about another man's horrific crime. "That's terrible!" Dave exclaimed. "Why, that man should die for what he did. Tell me, who is he?" That's when Pastor Nathan confronted the king, "David, you are the man." Dave confessed his sin in private to his pastor, who gave him the Good News: "The LORD has taken away your sin."

In 2 Samuel 12, we have a beautiful example of individual confession and absolution between a penitent and his pastor/prophet. God's ministers speak both Law and Gospel to large groups in public preaching and teaching. A sinner troubled by sin can hear that wonderful truth in a most intimate way through individual confession and absolution. Throughout the ages the church has often exercised the Office of the Keys through individual confession and absolution, also known as holy absolution. However, as with many of the church's responsibilities, this precious act has often been misapplied and neglected. The Roman Catholic Church, for example, required confession as a condition of being admitted to the Sacrament of the Altar. In so doing, they took a Gospel rite and made it into a law.

147

Worse yet, they made poor sinners try to enumerate all their misdeeds, and then they added works-righteousness to the absolution by specifying acts of penance. Many Christians were driven to the point of despair under this system, most notably Luther.

But with characteristic evangelical balance, Luther retained confession and absolution in the Reformation, simply purifying it of its abuses. Thus we find these words in the Augustana:

> Confession has not been abolished in our churches, for it is not customary to administer the body of Christ except to those who have previously been examined and absolved. The people are very diligently taught concerning faith in connection with absolution, a matter about which there has been profound silence before this time. Our people are taught to esteem absolution highly because it is the voice of God and is pronounced by God's command. The power of keys is praised, and people are reminded of the great consolation it brings to terrified consciences. (AC XXV 1–4)

In later centuries, however, Pietist ministers sought to eliminate the practice of individual confession and absolution between pastor and penitent. They associated this rite with the improper understanding and applications found in the Roman Catholic Church at that time. For example, acts of penance, including the purchase of indulgences and performance of good works, were required of penitents making confession to realize forgiveness of actual sins. Since earning forgiveness through acts of penance directly violates the doctrine of justification by grace through faith, Pietists dismissed the entire practice and tried to abolish its use.

Today many churches and pastors fall prey to the same type of thinking. They reason that since the Roman Catholic Church still employs a form of confession and absolution, it must be in conflict with the teachings of Scripture on justification.

Luther, however, spoke strongly against such thinking, praising the benefits of properly administered confession and absolution. In fact, Luther insisted that such a practice is necessary for a Christian congregation to help administer the Office of the Keys. Luther notes in the Large Catechism that any Christian who is honest about personal sin will automatically desire to participate in such activities where God's grace is found:

> Therefore, when I urge you to go to confession, I am simply urging you to be a Christian. If I bring you to this point, I have also brought you to confession. Those who really want to be good Christians, free from their sins, and happy in their conscience, already have the true hunger and thirst. They snatch at the bread just like a hunted hart, burning with heat and thirst, as Ps. 42:2 says, "As a hart longs for flowing streams, so longs my soul for Thee, O God." That is, as a hart trembles with eagerness for a fresh spring, so I yearn and tremble for God's Word, absolution, the sacrament, etc. In this way, you see, confession would be rightly taught, and such a desire and love for it would be aroused that people would come running after us to get it, more than we would like. (LC, Confession, 32–34)

Because I became aware of people's thirst for absolution when talking about conflict, I have suggested to conference hosts that individual confession and absolution be offered to the participants. I usually get a tentative response: "Well, we don't really do that here." I ask if they believe in the benefits of holy absolution. "Of course we do, but I don't think that people will come. They are just not used to it." After some encouragement, they capitulate, predicting that no one will participate.

Over and over, conference hosts are amazed when several people go to individual confession and absolution, especially when the audience is primarily made up of professional church workers. At the first conference I suggested this, penitents were standing in line waiting for the three confessors that were appointed. Many had to give up their place in line because they didn't want to miss the closing worship service. At the second conference where I encouraged this, people wrote in their evaluations that not enough opportunity was given for individual confession and absolution.

No list is kept of who goes to confession or not. However, some penitents themselves seek me out to report what they experienced, expressing thanks and joy for the opportunity. One pastor found me after he received individual absolution. Still shedding tears he exclaimed, "I never knew that forgiveness could be so powerful!" At another conference, during a question and answer session, a professional church worker expressed his deep appreciation for the opportunity to receive forgiveness in such a private way. "I am so refreshed. I had forgotten how wonderful forgiveness is for me. Thanks for making this available today!"

It is difficult to express in words the awesome benefit we receive from hearing the cherished news given to us privately through the words of our own pastor. And yet, today most Christians miss out on what should be a regular practice of the evangelizing pastor.

In addition to my own experiences, many others have shared how holy absolution shaped their lives. One retired businessman near death asked troubling questions about crooked people when his pastor visited him and his family in the hospital. Picking up on the cues, his pastor excused the family members to see if there was something his parishioner wanted to share in private. This man, a respected leader of his church, began to choke as he asked if those who cheated clients and employees could ever go to heaven. The conversation led to the man confessing a pattern of sins that troubled his conscience for years. Upon being absolved, tears overcame a man who was known for his stoic courage. He died a few days later, confident of his forgiveness in Christ and his place in heaven, though he knew he was undeserving on his own merits.

A Christian school principal suffered from years of addiction to Internet pornography, which was discovered by the school secretary. She uncovered the principal's extensive stash of saved pictures on the school's office computer while looking for some old files. The entire staff, school board, and the principal's wife reacted with shock, disgust, and anger. Destitute and considering suicide, he sought counsel from a neighboring pastor because his congregation was currently without a pastor. Pastor Roberts picked him up from his rural home and started driving toward the church on county roads. As the principal confessed his sin during the journey, expressing sorrow and despair, Pastor Roberts pulled the car over to the side of the road, placed a hand on his head, and absolved his sin. The contrite man wept nonstop for 10 minutes. In the months that followed he followed the counsel of his father/confessor, strengthened in the forgiveness of sins, and was reconciled to his wife. Eventually he was restored to ministry in a supervised setting.

Absolution comforts all sinners, not just those with sins we have labeled as disgusting, heinous, or criminal. From God's perspective, all our sins are disgusting, heinous, and criminal in view of His Law. In fact I have often speculated on how many of us Christians could avoid the painful consequences of long-term patterns of sin if we had only sought absolution in the earliest steps of our evil progression.

In church conflict interventions, the pastor on our reconciler team sometimes acquires permission to hear confession. Church leaders, including the pastors and teachers, come to confess sins of gossip, angry and hurtful words, denial of sin and conflict, running away rather than reconciling, and many more sins that give rise to the congregation's disputes. In addition, however, people use the opportunity to be absolved for sins against their spouses, children, employers, employees, and in other areas of their daily lives. Because all have sinned and fallen short of the glory of God, and since in our sinful nature we continue to sin daily, every one of us benefits from our pastor's private proclamation: "The Lord has taken away your sin because of Jesus' blood and righteousness. Go in peace."

Because this practice has fallen into such disuse in the church today, I have included a short form of confession and absolution from Luther's Small Catechism in the Appendix D for your easy reference. While Scripture does not command that we use such a rite, following a specific order can be consoling to the one confessing and to the one speaking absolution. The exposure of our sin to another, especially our pastor, is painful and humiliating. A short order, using words from Scripture, guides us in unfamiliar and dangerous territory. It also prevents a pastor from missing the main point: announcing God's forgiveness clearly and succinctly. A human confessor can be easily distracted by the surprise of an unexpected sin or the desire to provide guidance and counsel, and forget to absolve the sinner. Thus, a prepared order provides safeguard for both penitent and confessor, while still giving flexibility for specific circumstances.

Family Confession and Absolution

Married couples should confess and absolve each other's sins. Parents ought to forgive their children. Families can and should serve as ambassadors of reconciliation to each other.

Although I knew this from my childhood confirmation, I did not apply that knowledge in my own family for many years. Instead, I frequently resorted to my old Adam, using flight or assault in response.

One day my wife, Sonja, and I caught our teenage son David in a specific sin, which led to a major family confrontation. My pride, damaged from my son's apparent disregard for his Christian upbringing, quickly inflamed my anger, which erupted in my ranting, raving, and some tears. Sonja joined in, encouraged by her husband's poor model. Of course, David attempted to protect himself with denial, refusal to answer some questions, and loud retorts to unfair allegations. All in all, we demonstrated a poor example of a Christian family living as reconciled children of God.

When we stopped to take a breather from the fiery exchange, the thought crossed my mind, *As a Christian father, what am I to do?* In my heart, I knew that I botched it big time. Then I remembered. *Jesus died for this very purpose. Apply what you believe through absolving your son.*

I was stumped. *How do I absolve my son's sin? After all that we yelled at each other, how can I move into a more Christ-centered reaction?*

I reached for a resource that I knew provided an answer. We opened our personal copies of the hymnal to the order for Individual Confession and Absolution. I suggested to my family that this could serve as a pathway for us to respond to sin as God has shown His people. As we read our various parts in the rite, I had to change the words that referred to David's called and ordained pastor as his confessor, since I was his father but not his pastor. Our son confessed his sin, and I spoke God's forgiveness to him. We prayed together Psalm 51 and added other petitions at the end. We calmly discussed together what consequences would be appropriate for all concerned, and we ended with hugs of love. Reconciliation came through absolving our son of his sin.

Two years later our family experienced another disheartening event when Sonja and I discovered a different error our son had fallen into. My heart ached as I began to plot my verbal blows, and then I paused to remember our previous experience with absolution. I calmly confronted my son, allowing him to attempt to dig his own grave of self-justification for a few seconds. But I stood quietly firm, since the evidence was convicting, and told him that his mother and I would be waiting in the family room for his response. After several minutes he entered to calmly and specifically admit his guilt. I asked him, "David, how do you think we as your parents should respond?" His answer was immediate, "Dad, do you think we could go through that service of confession and forgiveness?"

Tears immediately swelled my eyes. My son understood. His assurance was found in the forgiveness of sins through his Savior, Jesus Christ. David's confession of faith inspired me and my wife, and together we celebrated life as forgiven sinners in words of confession and absolution.

A few months later, Sonja showed me a paper David had written for a high school project. The assignment was to describe someone he admired. David wrote about his parents and what he appreciated most about them. One of his main points centered on the assurance that his parents loved him and forgave him, no matter what he did. As a pastor once shared with me, I also exclaimed, "I never knew that forgiveness could be so powerful!"

Pastor David Poovey, one of my current pastors, surveyed the attitudes of his eighth grade confirmation students. He instructed them to prioritize the top ten answers to what makes a perfect parent. The choices included: letting me stay up late, letting me watch any movie or television program that I like, letting me wear whatever I want, letting me drive a car, letting me choose my friends, and forgiving me when I do wrong. These junior high kids identified the number one attribute of a perfect parent as "forgiving me when I do wrong." Our children cherish forgiveness.

Pastor Poovey begins wedding services with a general confession and absolution for all assembled (a copy of what he uses can be found in Appendix E). Here, the couple, their families, and guests all hear the Good News of God's forgiveness as together they celebrate the holy union of a new husband and wife. Then he explains that confession and forgiveness, before God and with each other, will help this new couple grow in their relationship as a married couple and as children of God. What a great way to begin your first moments of wedded life!

Imagine how Christian families could help transform the world if their lifestyle reflected their faith through regular confession and forgiveness. Because some may find it difficult to adapt the order for Individual Confession and Absolution for family use, I have provided one in Appendix F. I encourage your family to review it together and adapt it for your use. I pray that this is helpful to you as you consider how to confess sins and absolve one another as ambassadors of Christ living together as family.

Requirements for Hearers of Confession

Christians—and especially pastors—who hear another person's confession need to maintain certain disciplines.

Confidentiality is essential. The specific confession of a sinner in private must die with the confessor. Pastors vow to maintain the confidentiality of their office at their ordination. Christians entrusted by brothers and sisters with secret sins must also honor this same trust. In cases where the safety of others may be in question (such as the confession of a sex offender who continues to work with children), civil laws require reporting to proper authorities. However, the best way for this notification to take place avoids violating the confidentiality trust. If a sinner is repentant and has been forgiven, and if that person's condition puts others in danger, then the fruit of that person's repentance will include taking actions to protect all people involved. The confessor should offer to share that person's burden by accompanying the sinner to report to the appropriate authorities.

One who listens to others' confessions must also be a penitent who goes to confession. If anyone, pastor or other Christian, hears the confession of another without personally experiencing the humiliation and joy of private confession, that person may be easily tempted in several ways. First, the confessor may become self-righteous by comparison with the awful sin others confess.

This leads to sinful judging and condescending attitudes. A second danger is that the confessor may attempt to pry into the juicy details of the sin, feeding on the natural lusts that arise as he hears the story. Third, the confessor may be tempted to coldly treat the sinner as another clinical case, forgetting the shame and deep remorse that sinners sometimes experience over their sin and the inexpressible joy that forgiveness can bring in relief. This condescending attitude may lead the confessor to look down on the poor, pitiful creature that confessed. He may swell with pride at being the deliverer of peace.

Bonhoeffer qualifies hearers of confession:

> Anybody who has once been horrified by the dreadfulness of his own sin that nailed Jesus to the Cross will no longer be horrified by even the rankest sins of a brother. . . . Only the brother under the Cross can hear a confession. It is not experience of life but experience of the Cross that makes one a worthy hearer of confessions. (P. 118)

When employed as God's instruments for His peace, we sometimes witness the miracles that result from God's grace and power. A great temptation for any Christian leader is assuming credit for the work that God does through him. Hearing others' confessions and absolving sin in the name of Christ is powerful and potentially dangerous work.

Thus, St. Paul instructs ambassadors of the ministry of reconciliation: "We implore you on Christ's behalf: Be reconciled to God" (2 Corinthians 5:20).

13

Professing Faith in Public Confession and Forgiveness

In addition to forms of private confession, there are times when public confession is beneficial. When we confess our sins together in worship, we testify to our faith in Christ and glorify God. When one group sins against another, corporate confession and forgiveness work reconciliation just as they do between individuals. When one member sins against the community, the offender addresses the offended with public confession and gives the body a chance to restore him or her through forgiveness.

Corporate Confession and Forgiveness

Under this heading I want to highlight two different types of corporate confession. The first one, which is most familiar to Christians, is a general confession of sins during a regular worship service. The second one is the confession of one body to another.

According to Scripture, confession of sin and confession of faith are acts of worship. Recognizing the Psalter as a worship resource, note that many psalms include statements of confession, acknowledging our sinfulness before God and praising Him for His wonderful acts. Psalm 51 teaches that expressing our contrition is pleasing to our God: "The sacrifices of God are a broken spirit; a broken and contrite heart, O God, You will not despise" (v. 17). The Israelites confessed their corporate sins, sometimes as an assembly and sometimes through their leader (see 1 Samuel 7; Ezra 10; Nehemiah 1 and 9; Daniel 9). As New Testament crowds were baptized and confessed their faith in Christ, they also worshiped God as they confessed their sins. "Many of those who believed now came and openly confessed their evil deeds" (Acts 19:18).

General confession of sins with the announcement of forgiveness during a worship service can be a most salutary practice, but it can also serve as a convenient but feeble substitute for individual confession and forgiveness. Confession and forgiveness is always worthwhile because it applies the promise of God: your sins are forgiven. The practice of general confession during a worship service serves to proclaim the Gospel according to the command of Christ to go and make disciples. However, the general confession was never intended to replace the practice of individual confession and absolution. Individuals suffering from a secret sin miss the opportunity to name their sin out loud and receive God's forgiveness for personal assurance and comfort. Unfortunately, today many churches have totally neglected the wonderful gift of individual confession and absolution, believing that the general confession during worship is all that is necessary. Both individual and corporate confession and absolution should be parts of the church's regular ministries.

In addition to the corporate body of believers confessing their sins before God, another form of confession can occur when one group of believers confesses its sins to another.

At First Christian Middle School, Miss Johnson's eighth graders were studying the Lewis and Clark expedition. In small clusters, students prepared presentations to the whole school as final projects for the series. Creative juices flowed as the students built props in the halls to support their drama, but their excited voices and noisy activities disturbed other classes throughout the school. One after another, classroom doors were slammed shut, demonstrating irritation against Miss Johnson's class.

Although Miss Johnson could have justified her class's behavior on good intentions and unbridled enthusiasm, she recognized that she and her students caused offense. She brought her students together, and they examined their actions against Scripture. She led her students in drafting a class confession. With permission from individual teachers, the eighth graders filed into each room and read their prepared confession. Miss Johnson also confessed her lack of directing her students more carefully. Each teacher and class responded with the granting of forgiveness.

Faculty and students were all blessed by the confession of Miss Johnson's class and by the forgiveness shared. Pupils and teachers glorified God, served each other, and grew more Christlike through this opportunity. These ambassadors lived their faith in reconciliation.

In another case where our reconciler team assisted a congregation in conflict, we challenged the board of elders for their defensive position against many in the congregation. They had taken specific actions as a board that led to the termination of the church's pastor, and they had come under fire from many in their church. In a specially called congregational meeting, angry members resolved to remove every elder from his elected position. After extended debate, the elders felt exonerated when the motion to remove them was defeated, 56 to 54.

As our team met with the elders, we examined their attitudes and actions against specific Bible passages. We affirmed certain actions that were honorable, but we also showed them their faults. At first the elders were afraid to admit their wrongdoing, having narrowly escaped a hostile termination. But after some time, they came to understand their sin, and their self-righteous attitudes waned. During a meeting of all the church's leadership, the board stood in front of their peers and read a well-prepared confession. Unlike previous speeches, this statement identified specific actions and attitudes as sinful and offensive. This time they offered to step down as a consequence of their failure to act as spiritual leaders. Missing from their words was any attempt to justify or blame others.

The remaining leaders fell deeply quiet, unsure how to respond. With a little encouragement, the listeners read the words of absolution from their hymnals with solid conviction. Afterward, individuals who had previously launched verbal attacks against the board expressed their personal forgiveness as well. Later in the evening the leadership suggested that their elders share their reconciliation experience with the entire congregation, by confessing their sins during the next morning's worship service. Upon their confession, the rest of the leaders stood from their various pews and recited together the absolution. Pastor then invited the rest of the congregation to join in absolving their brothers. In the next congregational meeting, a vote of confidence in the board of elders was passed by a wide margin. Group confession and forgiveness is a great way to celebrate the ministry of reconciliation.

Individual Public Confession and Forgiveness

Occasionally, a member of the body of Christ commits a sin that offends the entire church. This may include a sin against the church itself, or it may include a public sin that brings shame upon the whole community. In such cases, sinner and church can benefit from an individual publicly confessing that sin before the entire group.

Steve had served in several leadership positions in his church and community. He was well respected and had received honors for his public service to the community. But one day people were appalled to learn that Steve had molested children.

Steve first admitted his crimes to his pastor in individual confession. Comforted and encouraged with the Gospel, he demonstrated fruits of repentance with confessions to the people he hurt most. With Pastor Morris by his side, he met separately with the two families whose children he had touched, and then he met with his wife, to confess his horrid sin. Next, Pastor Morris accompanied Steve as he reported the matter to civil authorities.

A number of events rapidly took place. Steve lost his job and was immediately removed from his leadership position in the church. Family services required him to leave his home until their investigation had been completed. Criminal charges were filed against him by the civil authorities.

Pastor Morris undertook the burdensome task of ministering to all of the hurting families, including Steve's. Processes were employed to protect the identities of the affected families for the sake of the children. Meanwhile, Steve struggled with depression while he waited for the inevitable consequences that would follow. The news media prepared to release reports on the unbelievable tragedy and the court case that would follow.

With his pastor's counsel, Steve decided to also seek forgiveness from his fellow church members in a public confession. On Sunday Pastor Morris announced that a special service of confession and absolution for one member would follow the regular worship service. Only congregational members were invited to attend.

The hymn "Jesus Sinners Will Receive" opened the service. Pastor Morris read Scripture passages that reminded the somber assembly of our Savior's purpose. All people are sinners. None of us can redeem ourselves, but God through Christ forgives us our sins so that all who believe in Jesus will be welcomed into heaven. Christ came to save sinners, such as St. Paul, who claimed to be the worst. Everyone quietly listened to the message, carefully digesting how these words applied to Steve and to themselves. As he introduced Steve, Pastor Morris stated that one of their own members had sinned against the entire church, and he desired to confess his sin before his brothers and sisters. Steve trembled as the words stumbled from his lips. He did not detail his specific acts of pedophilia, but he identified his sins of breaking trust with the congregation and bringing public shame upon the name of Christ and His church. He broke down as he acknowledged that he deserved nothing but God's wrath and judgment, and he asked for forgiveness for the sake of Jesus Christ, in whom he confessed his faith. Pastor Morris spoke God's forgiveness to him. Prayer and another hymn of God's grace followed.

Pastor then announced that Steve would be sitting in a private room, willing to talk to anyone who had something to say to him. He instructed the congregation that this may be the last opportunity to speak directly to Steve since he was heading to prison. He strictly exhorted members to not gossip about this event. If anyone had specific concerns about what happened, Pastor Morris urged them to speak directly to Steve or himself.

Nearly everyone present lined up to speak privately to Steve. Many cried with him and shared their personal forgiveness with him, although they made it clear that they did not condone his actions. Steve was taken aback when several members confessed some of their private sins to him, telling him that they, too, were sinners and in need of Christ's forgiveness.

Several years later an elder visited a long-term member of the church who declared, "I can't believe that the church leadership made Steve stand in front of the whole church to confess his sin!" The elder then shared, "It wasn't the leaders who forced Steve to confess. He wanted to. He sought the comfort that only the Gospel can give." The complaining member contemplated what the elder reported, and they discussed the great gift of forgiveness for addressing all the sin issues in our life. Steve's public confession of sin continued to impact the members of his church for many years.

When Individual Public Confession Is Appropriate

The public confession of an individual can provide healing for many, including the sinner and the body that she has offended. Forgiveness must follow a confession, as we discussed earlier in this book. However, one must use discretion to determine if a public event is appropriate.

Some individuals suffer weak faith, and they cannot face groups of people in confession. No one should be tortured to publicly confess when that person is not ready. Forcing confession in any situation exceeds our responsibility as ambassadors.

Not every sin should be publicly confessed, including those of leaders. It is not only impractical and unnecessary, but it is also impossible. As written earlier, we cannot confess every sin because we cannot know every sin.

A church leader is a sinner among many and thus

benefits from private absolution. Just like members, the pastor and leaders require confidentiality from their confessor. To regularly confess sins publicly before a group essentially eliminates protection of privacy.

In addition, if a leader uses the whole church as a regular confessor, that person will undermine personal credibility with those whose faith is immature and with unbelievers. On the other hand, church leaders must be careful to avoid acting or speaking like self-righteous Pharisees. Hypocrites are readily recognized and also lose credibility among others. Thus, it is appropriate to be vulnerable and open about one's weaknesses without confessing the details of one's sins. Further, it is beneficial for a church leader to readily admit fault after publicly offending the group and ask for forgiveness.

Public confession of sin is best employed when one has obviously or publicly sinned against the community. This provides an open way for the sin to be forgiven, and it discourages sinful gossip and slander. In addition, it demonstrates a public witness to unbelievers who judge the church for its leaders who fall.

A person considering a public confession will benefit from first confessing in private and receiving absolution. That person usually appreciates assistance from a Christian friend in preparing her thoughts. I suggest that the sinner take time to prepare, writing out the confession. (Review the "Seven A's of Confession" as summarized in Chapter 11 or more fully explained in Sande's book.) Confessing sin in public is stressful. Having a written statement guides the offender to say precisely what is intended and avoid unintentional slips.

When an individual plans to confess publicly, a church leader should be notified so that he can prepare to lead the group in proclaiming God's forgiveness. Although Christ directs His disciples to forgive those who repent, we are so unaccustomed to absolving sinners that in our surprise we forget how to respond to confession. Hymns, Bible reading, and prayers help set the stage for a group to hear an individual's confession and prepare them for forgiving the individual.

What about Consequences?

Although forgiveness removes the consequence of eternal damnation and restores relationships, earthly consequences may follow. For example, Scripture indicates that Moses disobeyed God and was forgiven, but he was forbidden from entering the Promised Land. In another case, King David confessed and was restored to God, but he suffered consequences of his sin, including death of the son born from his adultery and additional conflict within his family.

When a leader breaks trust with the church, he or she may lose that privilege of serving in that position, even though forgiveness is granted. Scripture provides strict requirements for pastors, elders, and teachers in the church (e.g., Ezekiel 34:1–16; 1 Timothy 3:1–13; James 3:1). Those who severely violate the authority entrusted to them may lose that privilege even though they are forgiven. A penitent leader who accepts the earthly consequences given him by his supervisor or congregation demonstrates fruit of repentance. On the other hand, the person or group who determines appropriate consequences for a fallen leader must be careful that consequences are appropriate for the offense, with considerations for both mercy and justice, and provide example and protection for the offender and for others who may be affected by the leader's actions.

In all cases, Christians living together under the cross remember that all have sinned, but all are forgiven through the blood of the Lamb.

14

Reconciliation: Not Just an Event

As I was describing the need for reconciliation to denominational leadership, one of the district supervisors asked, "How do we do a reconciliation event?"

Reconciliation is not a planned program but a lifestyle. Reconciliation through confession and forgiveness can be experienced in specific events, but our Lord never intended that His ministry be only reserved for special occasions.

We can demonstrate how our Christian faith separates us from the world by the way that we respond to sin. Our sinful nature tempts us to adopt the world's way of dealing with sin and miss the opportunity to share God's grace with one another.

Pastor Williams shook the foundations of his church one Sunday by a vivid demonstration of how unbiblical our lifestyles have become. Following the congregation's general confession of sin, he declared, "As a called and ordained servant of the Word, I announce to you that God says, 'That's okay. No problem. Forget it. You should be sorry. Don't ever do it again. I forgive you, but I don't want to have anything to do with you. Go in peace, but don't come back!'"

His people dropped their jaws, frozen in disbelief.

"What's the matter? Isn't that the way you respond to someone who apologizes to you? But you don't want your God to forgive you that way?"

This introduced Pastor Williams's sermon on forgiveness. Following his message, he properly absolved his members, who appreciated more than ever the precious treasure of God's love.

Several weeks later a young couple approached Pastor Williams, thanking him again for his unusual message on reconciliation.

"Pastor, you're helping change the culture of our home."

"What do you mean, Andy?"

"Last week Janet and I had one of our typical spats in the kitchen. But as we cooled down and regained our senses, we used a different way of speaking. We used words such as *I confess* and *I forgive*. You reminded us that as Christians, we have a new language to deal with wrongs. It's God's way for us to share the Good News with each other."

Sin is never *okay*. Sin is never *no problem*. There is only one cure for sin—forgiveness through our Lord Jesus Christ. What a privilege we have to serve as God's agents in sharing this Good News!

The living message of salvation was never meant to be employed only in worship services or crisis situations. For the ambassador of Christ, expressing words of reconciliation is one way we declare the marvelous deeds our God has done for us. In confession and forgiveness, we profess our faith and need for a Savior, and we share the Gospel with one another in practical, everyday experiences. We celebrate the death of the old Adam and our new life in Christ. We remember our Baptism and adoption as children of God. We glorify God as we say the words He taught us: *I confess. I forgive.*

Be a faithful ambassador of reconciliation. Live the message you believe and profess.

Then, with Isaiah, we will thank God for His special agents:

"How beautiful on the mountains are the feet of those who bring good news, who proclaim peace, who bring good tidings, who proclaim salvation, who say to Zion, 'Your God reigns!'" (Isaiah 52:7).

Appendix A

The Peacemaker's Pledge
A Commitment to Biblical Conflict Resolution

As people reconciled to God by the death and resurrection of Jesus Christ, we believe that we are called to respond to conflict in a way that is remarkably different from the way the world deals with conflict.[1] We also believe that conflict provides opportunities to glorify God, serve other people, and grow to be like Christ.[2] Therefore, in response to God's love and in reliance on His grace, we commit ourselves to respond to conflict according to the following principles:

Glorify God • Instead of focusing on our own desires or dwelling on what others may do, we will seek to please and honor God—by depending on His wisdom, power, and love; by faithfully obeying His commands; and by seeking to maintain a loving, merciful, and forgiving attitude.[3]

Get the log out of your own eye • Instead of attacking others or dwelling on their wrongs, we will take responsibility for our own contribution to conflicts—confessing our sins, asking God to help us change any attitudes and habits that lead to conflict, and seeking to repair any harm we have caused.[4]

Go and show your brother his fault • Instead of pretending that conflict doesn't exist or talking about others behind their backs, we will choose to overlook minor offenses, or we will talk directly and graciously with those whose offenses seem too serious to overlook. When a conflict with another Christian cannot be resolved in private, we will ask others in the body of Christ to help us settle the matter in a biblical manner.[5]

Go and be reconciled • Instead of accepting premature compromise or allowing relationships to wither, we will actively pursue genuine peace and reconciliation—forgiving others as God, for Christ's sake, has forgiven us, and seeking just and mutually beneficial solutions to our differences.[6]

By God's grace, we will apply these principles as a matter of stewardship, realizing that conflict is an opportunity, not an accident. We will remember that success, in God's eyes, is not a matter of specific results but of faithful, dependent obedience. And we will pray that our service as peacemakers brings praise to our Lord and leads others to know His infinite love.[7]

1: Matthew 5:9; Luke 6:27–36; Galatians 5:19–26.
2: Romans 8:28–29; 1 Corinthians 10:31–11:1; James 1:2–4.
3: Psalm 37:1–6; Mark 11:25; John 14:15; Romans 12:17–21; 1 Corinthians 10:31; Philippians 4:2–9; Colossians 3:1–4; James 3:17–18; 4:1–3; 1 Peter 2:12.
4: Proverbs 28:13; Matthew 7:3–5; Luke 19:8; Colossians 3:5–14; 1 John 1:8–9.
5: Matthew 18:15–20; 1 Corinthians 6:1–8; Galatians 6:1–2; Ephesians 4:29; 2 Timothy 2:24–26; James 5:9.
6: Matthew 5:23–24; 6:12; 7:12; Ephesians 4:1–3, 32; Philippians 2:3–4.
7: Matthew 25:14–21; John 13:34–35; Romans 12:18; 1 Peter 2:19; 4:19.

Appendix B

Questions for Examination

Based on the Ten Commandments, these questions help to examine oneself before confession or while in conflict with others. Although this list is not exhaustive, it does provide some personal reflection on how a person has sinned against God and others.

Confession may be preceded by a candid examination of yourself—your actions, motives, and nature (1 Corinthians 11:28). This examination leads you to speak the truth about yourself before the Lord. Like a mirror, these questions are designed to reflect the truth about you in the light of the Law (James 1:22–25). They expose not merely your sins, but the fact that you are unable "by nature to have true fear of God and true faith in God" (AC II 1–2). In this way, they encourage serious, thoughtful, and truthful self-examination so that you may heartily and sincerely confess, "God have mercy on me, a sinner" (Luke 18:13).

The First Commandment: You shall have no other gods.

What or whom do I fear most? (If my answer is something other than God, has this thing or person become a god to me?)

When a certain desire or expectation is not met, do I feel frustration, resentment, bitterness, or anger? (Do I crave something or someone else more than God? Then perhaps I worship the created more than the Creator.)

Am I sharply critical of others? (Am I simply discerning and loving others, attempting to help them with constructive change, or have I made myself to be god and judged others?)

Have I threatened others in any way? (If so, perhaps I have made myself to be god.)

Do I have the Lord God—Father, Son, and Holy Spirit—as my only and true God?

The Second Commandment: You shall not misuse the name of the Lord your God.

Do I curse, swear, use satanic arts, lie, or deceive by His name?

Do I call upon Him in every trouble, pray, praise, and give thanks?

Do I use God's name carelessly or thoughtlessly?

The Third Commandment: Remember the Sabbath Day by keeping it holy.

Do I despise preaching and God's Word by avoiding worship and Bible study?

Do I neglect the Gospel and Sacraments or make light of them when they are given?

Do I pray for my pastor and support his efforts to guard Christ's flock from error?

The Fourth Commandment: Honor your father and your mother.

Do I honor my father and mother, and other authorities (pastors, teachers, employers, supervisors, governmental leaders, etc.)?

Do I despise them or act disrespectfully toward anyone in authority?

Do I serve and obey them, love and cherish them?

Do I obey all the laws of the city, state, and country,

and pay for all my rightful share of all taxes?

Am I threatening, abusive, or overbearing to those who are under my charge?

The Fifth Commandment: You shall not murder.

Have I hurt or harmed my neighbor in his body?

Have I unjustly taken the life of anyone, born or unborn?

Do I hate anyone, or am I angry with anyone (see Matthew 5:21–22; 1 John 3:15)?

Have I lost my temper or injured my neighbor by thoughts, words, or deeds?

Am I abusive in word or deed toward my spouse, children, or anyone else?

Have I neglected to help and support my neighbor in every physical need?

The Sixth Commandment: You shall not commit adultery.

Do I lead a sexually pure and decent life in everything I say and do?

Have I reserved sexual intercourse for the pleasure and consolation of my spouse and, when God wills, for the procreation of children?

Have I held in highest regard God's gift of sexuality, or have I debased it in any way by my thoughts, words, or conduct?

Do I flee sexual immorality (lust, adultery, homosexual desires, self-gratification, pornography, etc.)?

The Seventh Commandment: You shall not steal.

Have I taken my neighbor's money or possessions, or gotten them in any dishonest way?

Do I help my neighbor to improve and protect his

possessions and income?

Do I cheat or otherwise seek to get what I have not earned?

Do I take care of what I have, pay what I owe, return what I borrow, and respect other people's property?

Do I give generously, or am I selfish, stingy, and greedy with my time and money, seeking to only serve my own interests?

Do I neglect or am I unfaithful to the responsibilities of my vocation and work?

Do I withhold my offerings to God as a way to force others in my church to change?

The Eighth Commandment: You shall not give false testimony against your neighbor.

Do I tell any falsehoods (lies, exaggerations, half-truths, etc.) about my neighbor, betray her, slander her, or hurt her reputation?

Do I defend him, speak well of him, and explain everything in the kindest way?

Do I gossip, listen to rumors, or take pleasure in talking about the faults or mistakes of anyone?

Do I defend others against false accusations?

Do I judge others without being duly authorized?

Do I speak the truth in love so that it covers a multitude of sins?

Do I use reckless or worthless words when speaking about others?

Do I use e-mail or other Internet communications as a way to break this commandment?

The Ninth Commandment: You shall not covet your neighbor's house.

Do I covet anything owned or enjoyed by my

neighbor?

Do I scheme to get what belongs to my neighbor or get it in a way that only appears right?

Do I help and serve my neighbor in keeping and protecting what is hers?

Am I discontent with what belongs to me?

Do I crave something better, different, or more than what God has given me?

Do I seek to satisfy the desires and appetites of my flesh? Am I greedy? Do I gamble? Am I a lewd dresser? Am I a glutton? Am I an alcoholic?

Have I sued or used other means to get something to which I am not entitled?

The Tenth Commandment: You shall not covet your neighbor's wife, or his manservant or maidservant, his ox or donkey, or anything that belongs to your neighbor.

Do I covet my neighbor's spouse, workers, or animals?

Do I entice or force them away from my neighbor or turn them against him?

Do I urge them to stay and do their duty?

Am I discontent with my spouse, family, vocation, job, or employees the Lord has given me?

Have I done anything to break up a friendship or marriage?

Have I encouraged someone to get a divorce?

Have I come between a child and her parents?

Am I contentious, or have I encouraged disharmony in my congregation, family, or workplace?

Am I manipulative or controlling?

Have I done all I could to mend or strengthen broken relationships?

Many of these questions are adapted or taken from work prepared by the Commission on Worship of The Lutheran Church—Missouri Synod (2001 and 2002) in preparation for a new hymnal or from The Peacemaker: A Biblical Guide to Resolving Personal Conflict by Ken Sande.

Appendix C

Words of Absolution from Scripture

When you forgive someone who has offended you, remind yourself and the other person that the real source of forgiveness is found in Jesus Christ. "I forgive you, _____, because God through Jesus has forgiven me and you."

God's Word is a means of grace that carries His authority. Comfort those you forgive by using direct quotes from Scripture, such as those listed below. Personalize the absolution by inserting the person's name in the verse. For example: "Shawn, Christ Himself bore your sins in His body on the tree, so that you might die to sins and live for righteousness; by Jesus' wounds, Shawn, you have been healed" (1 Peter 2:25).

"Blessed is he whose transgressions are forgiven, whose sins are covered. Blessed is the man whose sin the LORD does not count against him and in whose spirit is no deceit" (Psalm 32:1–2).

"[The Lord declares,] 'I will forgive their wickedness and will remember their sins no more'" (Jeremiah 31:34).

"[Jesus] was delivered over to death for our sins and was raised to life for our justification. Therefore, since we have been justified through faith, we have peace with God through our Lord Jesus Christ, through whom we have gained access by faith into this grace in which we now stand" (Romans 4:25–5:2).

"God made Him who had no sin to be sin for us, so that in Him we might become the righteousness of

God" (2 Corinthians 5:21).

"But because of His great love for us, God, who is rich in mercy, made us alive with Christ even when we were dead in transgressions—it is by grace you have been saved. And God raised us up with Christ and seated us with Him in the heavenly realms in Christ Jesus, in order that in the coming ages He might show the incomparable riches of His grace, expressed in His kindness to us in Christ Jesus. For it is by grace you have been saved, through faith—and this not from yourselves, it is the gift of God—not by works, so that no one can boast" (Ephesians 2:4–9).

"Once you were alienated from God and were enemies in your minds because of your evil behavior. But now He has reconciled you by Christ's physical body through death to present you holy in His sight, without blemish and free from accusation—if you continue in your faith, established and firm, not moved from the hope held out in the gospel" (Colossians 1:21–23).

"He Himself bore our sins in His body on the tree, so that we might die to sins and live for righteousness; by His wounds you have been healed" (1 Peter 2:25).

"If we claim to be without sin, we deceive ourselves and the truth is not in us. If we confess our sins, He is faithful and just and will forgive us our sins and purify us from all unrighteousness" (1 John 1:8–9).

"The LORD has taken away your sin" (2 Samuel 12:13)

Appendix D

Holy Absolution (With Your Pastor)

FROM LUTHER'S SMALL CATECHISM

"When I urge you to go to confession, I am simply urging you to be a Christian." (Large Catechism, Brief Exhortation 32)

You may prepare yourself by meditation on the Ten Commandments and by praying Psalm 6, 7, 13, 15, 51, 121, or 130. If you are not burdened with particular sins, do not trouble yourself or search for or invent other sins, thereby turning confession into a torture. Instead, mention one or two sins that you know and let that be enough.

When you are ready, kneel before the altar and say:

Pastor, please hear my confession and pronounce forgiveness in order to fulfill God's will.

Proceed.

I, a poor sinner, plead guilty before God of all sins.

In particular I confess before you that I have lived as if God did not matter and as if I mattered most.

My Lord's name I have not honored as I should; my worship and prayers have faltered.

I have not let His love have its way with me, and so my love for others has failed.

There are those whom I have hurt and those whom I failed to help.

My thoughts and desires have been soiled with sin.

If particular sins trouble you, you may confess specific sins by saying:

What troubles me particularly is that . . .

Confess whatever you have done against the commandments of God and your own place in life.

Then conclude by saying:

I am sorry for all of this and ask for grace. I want to do better.

God be merciful to you and strengthen your faith.

Amen.

Do you believe that my forgiveness is God's forgiveness?

Yes, Pastor.

Let it be done for you as you believe. In the stead and by the command of my Lord Jesus Christ I forgive you all your sins in the name of the Father and of the †　Son and of the Holy Spirit.

Amen.

The pastor will know additional Scripture passages with which to comfort and strengthen the faith of those who have great burdens of conscience or are sorrowful and distressed.

Then the pastor concludes:

Go in peace.

Amen.

The penitent may remain to say a prayer of thanksgiving. Psalm 30, 31, 32, 34, 103, or 118 is also appropriate.

Appendix E

A Wedding Prayer of Confession and Absolution

Pastor: In the name of the Father and of the Son and of the Holy Spirit.

Congregation: Amen.

Pastor: By reason of sin, many a cross has been laid upon the estate of marriage. Nevertheless, our gracious heavenly Father does not forsake His children in an estate so holy and acceptable to Him, but is ever present with His many blessings. As we come before our almighty God today to ask His blessing on this man and this woman and their marriage, and since we can only come to our Lord with repentant hearts, we now ask our Lord to bless us and <u>names</u> with the forgiveness of any sins as we say:

Congregation: O most merciful heavenly Father, who has given Your only-begotten Son to die for us, have mercy on us, and for Jesus' sake grant us remission of all our sins; and by Your Holy Spirit increase in us true knowledge of You and of Your will and true obedience to Your Word, to the end that by Your grace we may come to everlasting life; through Jesus Christ, our Lord. Amen.

Pastor: Almighty God, our heavenly Father, has had mercy on us and has given His only Son to die for us and for His sake forgives us all our sins. To them that believe on Jesus' name, He gives power to become the children of God and has promised them His Holy Spirit. He that believes and is baptized shall be saved. Grant this, Lord, to us all.

Congregation: Amen.

Appendix F

Family Confession and Forgiveness

Confession of sin is a private matter and should be kept confidential by the person hearing the confession and announcing God's forgiveness.* Christians are obligated to respect the confidential nature of a confession.

The penitent may prepare by meditating on the Ten Commandments and by praying Psalm 6, 7, 13, 15, 51, 121, or 130. If he is not burdened with particular sins, he should not trouble himself or search for or invent other sins, thereby turning confession into a torture. Instead, he should mention one or two particular sins that trouble him and let that be enough.

When he is ready, the penitent says:

_____ **(Father, mother, husband, wife, brother, sister, son, or daughter), please hear my confession and pronounce God's forgiveness in order to fulfill God's will.**

Please continue.

I, a poor sinner, plead guilty before God of all sins.

In particular I confess before you that I have lived as if God did not matter and as if I mattered most.

My Lord's name I have not honored as I should; my worship and prayers have faltered.

I have not let His love have its way with me, and so my love for others has failed.

There are those whom I have hurt and those whom I failed to help.

My thoughts and desires have been soiled with sin.

If particular sins trouble you, you may confess specific sins by saying:

What troubles me particularly is that . . .

Confess whatever you have done against the commandments of God and your own place in life.

If you have sinned against the person hearing confession, you may also say:

I have not only sinned against God, but I have also sinned against you and seek your personal forgiveness.

Then conclude by saying:

I am sorry for all of this and ask for grace. I want to do better.

God be merciful to you and strengthen your faith.

Amen.

Do you believe that God's promises of forgiveness given in Holy Scripture are written for all of God's children, including you?

I do.

Then listen to God's Word and let it be done for you as you believe.

In 1 John 1:9 God promises: "If we confess our sins, [God] is faithful and just and will forgive us our sins and purify us from all unrighteousness."

In Jeremiah 31:34 the Lord declares: "I will forgive [your] wickedness and will remember [your] sins no more."

In Romans 4:25–5:2 God wrote through St. Paul: "[Jesus] was delivered over to death for [your] sins and was raised to life for [your] justification. Therefore, since

[you] have been justified through faith, [you] have peace with God through our Lord Jesus Christ, through whom [you] have gained access by faith into this grace in which [you] now stand."

Therefore, my _____ (son, daughter, wife, husband, brother, sister, father, or mother), believe this Good News: For Jesus' sake God forgives you all your sins, in the name of the Father and of the † Son and of the Holy Spirit.

Amen.

If the penitent has also asked for forgiveness from the person hearing the confession, these words should also be spoken:

As God through Christ has forgiven both you and me, I also forgive you your sins against me.

Amen.

May the peace of God, which transcends all human understanding, guard our hearts and minds in Christ Jesus.

Amen.

A prayer of thanksgiving may follow. Psalm 30, 31, 32, 34, 103, or 118 is also appropriate.

The one hearing confession may know additional Scripture passages with which to comfort and strengthen the faith of those who have great burdens of conscience or are sorrowful and distressed.

*Exceptions may be required by Scripture (for manifest unrepentance) or by civil authorities (such as sexual crimes against children).

Bibliography

Barry, A. L. *Unchanging Truth in Changing Times: The Complete Collection of the What About Pamphlets*. St. Louis: The Lutheran Church—Missouri Synod, 2001.

Bonhoeffer, Dietrich. *Life Together*. San Francisco: Harper & Row, 1954.

Korby, Kenneth. "Confession and Absolution." Audiotaped workshop held at Concordia Catechetical Academy of Peace Lutheran Church, Sussex, Wis.

Lutheran Worship. St. Louis: Concordia Publishing House, 1982.

Luther's Small Catechism with Explanation. St. Louis: Concordia Publishing House, 1991.

Matzat, Don. *Christ Esteem: Where the Search For Self-Esteem Ends*. Eugene, Oregon: Harvest House, 1990.

Sande, Ken. *The Peacemaker: A Biblical Guide to Resolving Personal Conflict*. 2nd ed. Grand Rapids: Baker Books, 1997.

Sande, Ken. "The Peacemaker Seminar." Audiotaped seminar. Billings, Montana: Peacemaker Ministries, 2000.

Sande, Ken, and Ted Kober. *Guiding People through Conflict*. Billings, Montana: Peacemaker Ministries, 1998.

Senkbeil, Harold L. *Dying to Live: The Power of Forgiveness*. St. Louis: Concordia Publishing House, 1994.

Walther, C. F. W. *The Proper Distinction Between Law and Gospel*. Translated by W. H. T. Dau. St. Louis: Concordia Publishing House, 1929.

Welch, Edward T. *Addictions: A Banquet in the Grave.* Phillipsburg, New Jersey: P & R Publishing, 2001.

Other Resources

Several resources are available to help equip church leaders in the ministry of reconciliation. Numerous resources on peacemaking are available from Concordia Publishing House (CPH). *Here We Stand* by Hermann Sasse gives a general outline of the authentic Lutheran approach to ministry, which includes a strong emphasis on confession and the Lord's Supper. Harold L. Senkbeil's *Dying to Live* is a detailed description of the power of forgiveness in the Christian life. Also worth a look are the very helpful documents from the CTCR (Commission on Theology and Church Relations of the Lutheran Church—Missouri Synod). "Church Discipline" outlines biblical and confessional principles for dealing with congregational conflict. "The Pastor-Penitent Relationship" deals directly with the practice of private confession. *Joy in the Parish* by Charles Knippel shows how disfunctional congregations and pastors can find wellness in Christ and contains a section on confession and absolution. Of interest also will be the new series The Lutheran Difference, which examines the Lutheran approach to different topics and compares it with those of other denominations. Available now is *Confession* by Kory Maas.

Peacemaker Ministries also offers Bible studies (e.g., *Responding to Conflict Confessionally* by Ken Sande and Ted Kober) and other resources. Leaders can be introduced to coaching others or mediating disputes in the book *Guiding People through Conflict* by Sande and Kober.

Basic education for preparing people to coach and mediate is available through Peacemaker Ministries' *Reconciler Training Course* and *Reconciler Practicum,* and advance training is available through the *Conciliator Certification*™ program offered by the Institute for Christian Conciliation (ICC), a division of Peacemaker Ministries. The ICC assists Christians in specific conflicts through coaching, mediation, and arbitration services, and conflicted churches can benefit from intervention services. *Managing Conflict in Your Church,* an audiotaped seminar and manual by Ken Sande, provides instruction, model bylaws, and other forms for churches to prevent conflict, reduce legal liability, and organize for biblical peacemaking. Numerous articles and teaching principles are available for free downloading from the Peacemaker Ministries Web site at www.hispeace.org.

For more information, review the references listed in this book or contact CPH (1-800-325-3381 or www.cph.org) or Peacemaker Ministries (1-800-711-7118 or www.hispeace.org).